GAVIN…*GONE*

Turning Pain into Purpose to Create a Legacy

By
RITA GLADDING

Defining Moments Press, Inc.

Copyright © Rita Gladding, 2022

All rights reserved. No part of this book may be reproduced in any form without permission in writing from the author.

Disclaimer

No part of this publication may be reproduced or transmitted in any form or by any means, mechanical or electronic, including photocopying or recording, or by any information storage and retrieval system, or transmitted by email without permission in writing from the author.

Neither the author nor the publisher assumes any responsibility for errors, omissions, or contrary interpretations of the subject matter herein. Any perceived slight of any individual or organization is purely unintentional.

Brand and product names are trademarks or registered trademarks of their respective owners.

Defining Moments ™ is a registered Trademark

Cover Design: 99 Designs

Editing: Joy Montgomery

TABLE OF CONTENTS

DEDICATION

These chapters are dedicated to Carter and Isla Gladding
who carry Gavin's magic and messages within them.
Love,
Your Cha Cha

PREFACE

Rita Gladding's name and persona illuminate the darkened night sky like a brightly lit neon billboard. She is a fierce and virtuous leader, revered and loved in the community we both call home.

For years I admired from afar her hands-on approach to life, her unwavering and indomitable spirit, the down to earth ways she tackled issues and challenges. A woman with fire in her eyes – the kind of flame that makes things happen with passion and purpose. Simply put: she is a human firecracker.

When the news of her son Gavin's death hit the airwaves and front pages of the newspaper, an entire community grieved. The more we learned about Gavin's life, his impact and imprint upon the lives of young people around the world, the more senseless his death became.

On a late fall morning, I woke up knowing I had to see Gavin's mother, make eye contact, wrap my arms around her, share a grieving mom's heart and simply lean in. Fourteen years earlier I had lost my son, Alex, so I wanted her to know she was in for the most grueling journey of her lifetime. How can a mother go on without her son?

Without hesitation she informed me she had important business to tend to. While sitting with this woman, I witnessed her unrelenting determination to seek justice for her son's killer. In the countless months that followed, behind continuing headlines and editorials, newscasts and media briefings, caravan travels to the California Legislature, there she was – this extraordinary woman. She towered in focus and stature to not only seek justice, but in doing so – sharing Gavin's life with the world.

We began meeting to craft the story you are about to read. I did little, really – besides admire her from the sidelines, cheer her on, and weep while reading a commentary no mother should ever have to write. But in Rita's words, writing this story was non-negotiable. Losing Gavin ignited a flame inside his mother's heart that will never be extinguished.

In the final months of book writing, we occasionally met at a charming local hangout called Sierra Nuthouse. Over a glass of Chardonnay or Prosecco, we came to realize we were two women much greater than the sum of our broken parts – we had become sisters for life. As you venture into these pages, you will experience a vast range of emotions – from shock and horror, anger, and frustration, to deep and unimaginable sorrow. But make no mistake, in its purest essence this book is about the power of love and humankind. And I promise – it will leave you breathless.

Armen Bacon
Author of "Griefland: An Intimate Portrait of Love, Loss and Unlikely Friendship"

PROLOGUE

All of our lives are filled with an abundance of numbers, dates and statistics to remember, revisit, and ponder. I live with a tickertape of very personal numbers running through my mind.

My son, Gavin Gladding, was killed by a hit-and-run driver on September 16, 2018, while training for a marathon.

This is the story of strength, hope and the courage to forge onward to make Gavin's life and death meaningful. Although tragedy and death are part of this story, this is not about grief alone. After Gavin's passing, our family set out to find a route to healing. Purposely, forgiveness has also become a portion of our lives. It won't change what happened, but it can change what we hope to be Gavin's legacy.

Details of Gavin's death, along with our pursuit to bring justice for other California families disrupted by hit-and-run drivers who tragically ended the life of their family member, follows. It is a demonstration of how our commitment and conviction led us to peace.

The timeline of Gavin's short life totals forty-three years, four months, and three days but he made his years count and impacted so many people along the way.

Here is a breakdown of what he managed to accomplish during his 43 years on this earth.

Time spent earning a Bachelor of Science Degree in Environmental Science at University of Santa Barbara: five years.

Time spent volunteering in the Peace Corps assigned to live in The Gambia, West Africa: two years and two months.

Time spent married to Susan: fourteen years, eleven days.

Time spent with son, Carter: ten years, nine months, eleven days.

Time spent with daughter, Isla: eight years, four months, twenty-two days.

Time spent working for the San Joaquin River Parkway Conservancy and Trust in Fresno: 12 years.

Time spent securing a teaching credential and Masters in School Administration: 2.5 years.

Time spent teaching science: nine years.

Time spent as Vice Principal of Fort Washington Elementary School: two years, one month and ten days.

Date of the final service to honor him: September 24, 2018.

"Abdoulraxman" was the name given to Gavin by the villagers of Charmen, The Gambia. The Peace Corps assigned him to lead a beekeeping farm to generate income for that hamlet. In their native language of Wolof Abdoulraxman means "Messenger from God."

I don't know exactly what the villagers heard or wanted to hear from this messenger. I will never know for sure. However, since Gavin's death I keep wondering what messages he would have delivered if he had lived a full lifetime? I also wonder what message he has delivered upon his death.

I am left only with my own speculation and very personal perspective. My conclusions exemplify keeping alive the magnetism he shared. I persist in breathing the conviction his messages of peace, hope, equality, and happiness for his fellowmen will by no means allow his memory to be erased from the minds of all who knew him and read this book.

Rita Gladding

CHAPTER ONE
EVERYDAY STILL FEELS LIKE THE FIRST DAY

"May he rest in peace; may God grant the reuniting of him with his family in Heaven." Maryann – Student at Clovis West High School
Except from He Loved Us

On Sunday, September 16, 2018, my husband, Gary, and I ascended over the Grapevine into the San Joaquin Valley, returning home from visiting friends in Southern California. A beautiful clear, blue-skied morning spread the Valley out in front of us. Both of us were in a somber mood and there was an unusual silence between us. On the road by 6 a.m., we were returning to the valley to attend the funeral for a dear friend. My phone rang at 7:42 am. It was Gabrielle, our daughter, who I call Mimmie as a pet name. Knowing that she is an early riser, her morning phone call was not unusual. As I picked up the call I heard background noises from the road. She was traveling somewhere.

I answered cheerfully, innocently. "Hi, Mimmie! What's happening?" She immediately cut me off. "There's been an accident," she said. "It's Gavin." Her voice sounded shaky. She was talking very fast. Listening, I immediately discerned that the necessity of saying these words to us was causing her great pain. In that single split second my body stiffened, my chest tightened, my breathing became labored. And my heart sank to a depth I had never encountered before. The next sound I heard was Susan, our daughter-in-law, crying in the background. Gabrielle offered no other details except, "Come immediately to the emergency room at Community Regional Medical Center downtown, do not go home."

We gasped as screams began to rise from our throats. Gary and I spent the next three hours on the road left with only the last words spoken by our daughter, "*Do not go home.*" I grabbed my Rosary from the back seat – gifted by my friend, Marge, who brought it home to me from the Vatican. Blessed by Pope Francis. A numbness overcame me. There has never been a longer trip home. For the next three hours Gary and I text friends for prayers. My first text asked for prayers from Monsignor Rob at St. Anthony of Padua Catholic Church in Fresno, where I volunteer as a Eucharistic Minister. There was an accident. Monsignor responded immediately. Yes, he would pray for Gavin.

As we arrived at Community Regional Medical Center at 11:30 a.m., two social workers meet us in the hectic emergency entrance driveway. The looks on their faces shook me to the core. So much so, that I jumped out of the car as it was still moving. They explain that they're taking me to a "quiet room." I walk what seems like a two-sided gauntlet, passing nurses in the ER. Seeing the looks on their faces, I panic. Faces filled with dread. Faces that say, "Here comes The Mother." Several staff members avert my eyes completely. I plead to see my son. Where are Gabrielle and Susan? They must be comforting Gavin at that very moment. Still, I have not allowed the notion that this accident is serious to enter my head. Gavin is close, I can feel him. Perhaps in an operating room receiving the help he must need. God couldn't have wanted him already, couldn't have taken him so soon.

I turned around in an empty brightly lit florescent room to meet a young doctor who says, "Rita, your son was unresponsive at the accident site. He is brain dead. We were waiting for you to call time of death." Shaking, I fall to my knees. Gasping for air, I collapse to the shiny waxed floor screaming, screaming, then screaming louder. My only question is, "Did he suffer?" The ER doctor says, "No." I pray to God he is telling me the truth. I learn later that the doctor was the same age as Gavin. His children were the same age as Gavin's. He was visibly shaken. It took me weeks to understand what a terrible burden had been put on the shoulders of this man. My heart broke again – this time for the doctor who could not save Gavin.

Gary entered the room, took one look at me, immediately understood, and began wailing. Susan and Gabrielle came in, seeming calm beyond reason – numb. They'd had several hours to process the accident, but I still refused to believe what I've been told. I plead with the doctor, "Was there nothing that could have been done? No surgery? Stitches to hold his head together? Tape? Anything?!" I am told his injuries were too severe.

This is impossible. Unfathomable. This just doesn't happen. It can't happen. We are asked if we wanted to see Gavin. We enter a dimly lit ER room. There he is alone on a hospital table wrapped up like a mummy. Blood droplets are on the floor. Gavin's blood. There are blood-soaked sheets. His head is wrapped in bandages, but he has not a mark on his face. I approach, touch his shoulder, and begin weeping. He has a drain coming out of his mouth, there is a machine droning on beside him. The sight of other tubes projecting from his body will never diminish. He still has some color in his face, but he is cold to my touch.

In the darkened room there are sounds of people coming in and out. We say a prayer, the Our Father. I begin to say a Rosary with the beads I'd been clutching since the first phone call. With all eyes glued on Gavin, I pray for his next breath.

It isn't until my sweet, dear friend Kelly comes in weeping, followed by Monsignor Rob, that I realize the scene playing out in front of us is real. The first words Monsignor says to me are, "Rita, this isn't in the natural order of things. Parents before their children." He blesses Gavin. I still continue to fantasize that this isn't real. It has to be some sort of nightmare. Gavin cannot be gone from us, from this planet. "Dear God," I pray again, "please let him open his eyes." Slowly, a cold stark reality sets in. That is when I know Gavin has already ascended above. As the nurses ushered us out, Susan turns to ask for his wedding ring. We all stand frozen outside the curtain that separates us from him. His ring is handed to Susan delicately by a silent nurse who knows that there is nothing more she can say. Still numb, drenched in tears, we leave Gavin now forever, walking silently down the sterile halls and out the automatic glass doors.

Never in any of those agonizing last moments, standing vigil beside Gavin, did I ever wonder why he was taken. I knew exactly where he was. Raised in a small town in New Jersey, in an Italian family of devout Catholics, Mass every Sunday was a regular event. The biggest regret my parents had was not being financially able to have us attend the neighborhood Catholic grade school. I enjoyed Sunday Mass and the religious instruction resonated with my soul. I was quiet and attentive. I found it to be the only time I was ever a model student in any classroom.

As a woman of great faith, I knew Gavin was with the One that needs him most. It is a part of His greater plan. I have felt Gavin's fate all along. Deep inside me, I have known since May 13, 1975, that God wanted him. God silently sought after him from the first minute he entered this world. It was a greater part of His plan. Those left behind would forever suffer the loss of this kind human being, but God sought Gavin for a higher purpose. Required him in Heaven. Chose him that morning because He wanted the finest to join him

Born in Houston, Texas, Gavin struggled to enter this world. On the humid spring morning of his day of birth, we left our four-year-old daughter Gabrielle with my father, affectionately referred to as Poppy, while Gary drove me to the hospital by way of the backroads to avoid traffic. I sat back into the stiff seat of our blue Toyota and watched the night bloom into a beautiful day. I had felt sure that my second pregnancy was going to be much easier than the first. Diagnosed with Gestational Diabetes during my first pregnancy carrying Gabrielle, I knew the road ahead would be fraught with problems. I was ready for the challenges. High blood sugar, 50-pound weight gain, a baby that could weigh as much as ten pounds. I would take it in stride again. Knowing the joy that Gabrielle's birth brought to our lives, I knew every difficult moment would be worth it.

This time, immediately after our arrival at the hospital, nurses began to suspect something was wrong. I'm being attended to by five nurses plus three doctors. A Pediatrician waited outside the delivery room. There were identifiable problems. The baby's heart was skipping beats. Anesthesia was not working. Gary was dressed in green scrubs, blending into the green wall he leaned against. Looks of anxiety spread across the faces of staff in the delivery room. But nothing compared to my inconceivable feeling that something could happen to this baby. My baby.

The terrible heaviness hanging over all of us was the reality that gestational diabetic mothers have a high incidence of still-born babies. The placenta simply "plays out" during the last weeks of gestation. Eight months into my pregnancy, I was warned to be on the lookout for a lack of movement within me for any extended period. I wasn't actually frightened, more accurately I felt that caution would need to be my partner for the next month. Gary saw to it that I was never alone. We knew exactly the due date for this baby. We didn't know the gender but had pinpointed when forty weeks

19

would pass.

The day before my anticipated due date, my doctor ordered an ultrasound. You haven't lived until you are forced to drink a gallon of water when you're nine months pregnant. Tests confirmed that the circumference of baby's head was large enough to schedule a C-section for the following day. As God planned, I went into spontaneous labor that night. We reached the hospital at 6:45 the next morning. I was dilated to eight centimeters. Okay, we were going to have this baby soon, very soon.

The scurrying around me begins. More nurses, another anesthesiologist, Gary still green as the wall. Machines roll in. Tubes attached to my belly. Sensing that something was terribly wrong, Gary was ushered out of the tiny delivery room. I was conscious, but totally unconscious in those moments. Frozen. Staring at a clock that didn't seem to move, I realized there still was a storm of people surrounding me. All moving. Doing what? I'm not sure. I'm sure I prayed, but have no recollection of those prayers, just that the clock didn't appear to be moving forward. And the pain of childbirth is what everyone said it would be. Excruciating, not numbing. Every fiber in my being was aware of the trauma it was being subjected to.

At 9:57 a.m., amidst cheers from all present, a fat baby was pulled from me with the umbilical cord knotted three times. I knew this was not a terribly unusual occurrence, clearly Gavin had already been trying to explore. But the bigger problem was that the cord connecting the two of us was also tangled and wrapped around the baby's neck and stomach more than several times. That explained the irregular heartbeat. My baby was just trying to breathe. A fabric panel had been hung so I wasn't able to watch the delivery, but I'm told the doctor quickly unraveled the baby and announced that we'd had a boy. A few seconds later, I hear his cries. I flail my arms around until the nurses are forced to restrain me. Those stupid lifesaving tubes were still attached to my body.

I still hadn't seen my baby boy, but I heard him. I also heard the doctor say to Gary, "Good thing she had a fast labor. We would have lost this one for sure." It was then that I first had the unsettling thought that God wanted my little boy. An unimaginable tug of war begins. God may want him, but his mother wanted him more. I didn't understand God's plan then. This boy possessed something special that our planet needed, that must be shared with humankind: "Gavin's Magic." It definitely was God's plan. Gavin remained for 43 years, four months and three days in this world, but it wasn't enough time for me.

Over the years, I had randomly wondered how parents might feel about the night their child dies. How awful it must be. I could finally grasp why that thought had been reentering my mind for so many years. The night your child dies is like no other night you will ever encounter. A night you will never understand or be able to explain. What happened when we arrived home from the hospital on that beautiful Sunday afternoon is mostly just a blur. I was beginning to enter a state of shock that lasted for...well, it still goes on today. Why was everyone surrounding us? Sobbing and hugging. Somehow I was outside my body, viewing this scene with wide open eyes, but seeing nothing. As everyone got fuzzier, I remember clutching my Rosary, rocking back and forth on the sofa, and screaming. Gary was with some of our friends in the kitchen. I could hear him sobbing. A sound unfamiliar to me. Still refusing to believe Gavin had been killed, my clearest recollection is that most who were present that day joined hands in a circle while a close friend of ours (also named Gary), prayed with us. He asked the Lord to comfort our souls. To this day I don't believe this band of friends understood that I was only still standing because they were holding me up.

Later that night, in my semi-hysterical, frenetic state, I ran through the house grabbing every picture displayed of Gavin. There are many. I positioned them on my bed, sprinkled each with Holy Water from our trip to Lourdes, France. Spread out were all the photos in chronological order starting with the picture of him at three months, then 18 months old, then two years old, three years old, four years old. Included in the collection was a volleyball championship picture from Bullard High School when he was a senior, photos from UCSB taken when he held offices, in the Sigma Chi Fraternity house. I gazed at my favorite pictures of him in The Gambia, my favorite wedding picture of Susan and Gavin, Christmas group pictures spanning several years. My only disappointment was not being able to find his pictures with Santa that night. I carefully pack them away after Christmas each year. I crawled into bed surrounded by his images. Sleep would not come that night. Gavin was never coming home again. I know this for certain. Reality was sinking in. It wrenched my entire being.

On September 17, 2018, the first entire day that Gavin no longer walked this Earth, I arose at ten minutes before six a.m. I walked out onto our front lawn, starring up at the sky. I wanted to see how the sky looked at 5:58 a.m. the day before during Gavin's last moments. It was beautiful – still not completely light, but the sun was beginning to brighten everything. A serene calmness overtook me. No tears were shed. I will be eternally grateful to know that the sun was shining when he took his last steps and breaths.

Behind every thought and breath on the first horrendous night without Gavin was the lingering question: Would we ever discover who hit him and then ran? I prayed we would. Sometime earlier, on the Sunday afternoon of the accident, news reports began to surface. The sequence of events of the crash were blasted out by the media. Eyewitnesses had been running about 20 feet behind Gavin. They had seen Gavin get struck, fly through the air, and crash down on the side of the road. They watched the truck that mowed him down spin 360 degrees across the road. They witnessed the truck stop, straighten, and speed away. Damage to the pickup truck was so extensive that news anchors used drawings of what the truck could look like during broadcasts asking anyone who had seen this severely damaged vehicle to please come forward. Enormous amounts of broken glass covered with Gavin's blood littered Friant Road.

Whoever swept their headlights over Gavin's body that morning chose to leave him there. They chose not to stop. They weren't concerned that whomever they struck could still be alive. Although many years have passed, I am still conscious of the fact that Gavin could have died alone but didn't. The runners behind him were eyewitnesses to the crash. When the first runner reached him, he was still breathing. With a heavy heart I admit I have never contacted the woman who ran to his aid. Deep within my innermost self, I just can't accept the description I would receive. Later it was confirmed – he died at the scene. Hit-and-run. His magic was finished. Gavin *gone.*

Our highest priority would now become the steps needed to keep his memory alive. His earthly life had ended abruptly, but Gavin's existence was so much more. The footprint he left behind was large. As his students agreed in *He Loved Us – Stories of Mr. Gladding by the Students Who Loved Him,* he was "an inspiration and role model" to his students. A perfect example is written by his student, Alexandra: "One time, he was teaching us about the axis and rotation of the Earth and how that effects our climate. He could tell the class was confused so he brought all of us outside and we got into a big circle. In the center of the circle, he assigned someone to be the sun. Then he stuck his arm up saying he was the earth, and his arm was the 23 tilt on the earth's axis. He ran around our big circle, which made the whole class laugh, all the while exclaiming to us that when the earth is in this specific position relative to the sun it would be summer, winter, spring or fall in the northern hemisphere. Then he got all of us to be the earth and run around the circle. It felt silly, in a good way, and it will be a cherished memory that I will never forget." Gavin breathed and spread wonderment.

CHAPTER TWO
FIVE DAYS OF SILENCE

"When I first heard the news of his death I just sat down and cried for a while. I don't think I'll ever be able to understand why bad things happen to the best people in the world".
Brittany – Student at Clovis West High School
Excerpt from He Loved Us

For the five days following Gavin's sudden death, we were joined in mourning and prayer as an entire community hoped his killer would be found. Gavin had never arrived to join his friends for their Sunday morning golf game. He was never able to say goodbye to anyone. As a woman of faith, I believe and am comfortable with the concept that God has a plan for each of His children. This, I believe, was God's plan for His child and mine. It is as if Gavin fell right into God's blueprint for his life. No fuss, no lingering goodbyes. Gavin had deep emotions connected to every person he knew. To have actually uttered final goodbyes would have been devastating for him. He was a pure soul that couldn't abide transporting sadness upon the ones he loved, farewells that would have torn all who treasured him apart. Goodbyes that couldn't ever be properly said in any case. In God's infinite wisdom, He knew to snatch Gavin up without allowing him to impart final words.

Several days after the accident, I insisted my husband take me to the crash site. Gary never got out of the car. I stood on the hot black pavement picking up pieces of broken glass from the road as speeding cars, late for work in town, farmer's banging by in their rattily pick-up trucks, and over-sized wide trucks full of gravel from the nearby quarry pit roared past. They were mostly unaware of my presence, distracted by their own singular lives. I had a visual image of what it must have been like for Gavin running that morning. Struck from behind, he was unaware of the approaching truck that would take his life. I felt vulnerable but not afraid. For me to stand in the exact spot where he had stood, with my back to the oncoming flood of cars and trucks, was cathartic. Though most of the vehicles flew by, several cars slowed to wave at me. They knew who I was. I sprinkled the crash site with holy water from Lourdes and got back in the car.

A silence fell over the car. Gary and I said nothing to each other. The crash site, as we began to refer to the side of the road where Gavin took his last breath, became a place of pain for Gary. For me, it was the sacred ground representing the last minutes of my son's life. I feel peace standing there. In these ensuing years, many bicycle riders have stopped to talk to me. Cars and trucks have pulled off the road to speak to me, express their angriness. Media coverage was extensive in our San Joaquin Valley, Gavin's name was on the tip of many tongues. Still to this day, Gary remains inside the car as I frequently add flowers or balloons to the ongoing roadside memorial.

As the reality of our loss began to take hold of each of the members of our family and the community, the California Highway Patrol launched an extensive search for both the killer and the pick-up truck. As five days passed our family also continued praying. A press conference was broadcast live from CHP headquarters. My son-in-law, Garrett, made a plea to the community to come forward with anything that might ease our suffering. "We know that whoever did this is sorry," he said. "If it was an accident, please come forward." We prayed for this to be true, that whoever killed Gavin was living with great regret and repentance. I could not help but wonder if Gavin's killer and those who were hiding him, were watching the TV coverage. A man's life was taken. Were they consciously grieving? Was the killer rerunning a constant silent film within his head? When he closed his eyes could he see the after image of the scene of the accident, a silent replay except for the thunderous sound of Gavin's body hurtling through the air as the truck hit him? I wanted to believe that the culprit was home weeping and atoning for what he'd done while he tried to find a way to come forward and confess. Lead by faith and belief in Gavin's spirit, I did believe this.

We waited; each day filled with unspeakable emotions. Our grief was compounded with mystery. Who killed Gavin? Who is this person who was able to strike down another human being and then drive away, leaving a man lying on the side of the road, not knowing if he was alive or dead? Are there people without hearts or souls? Finding that prospect hard to comprehend, we continued to beg for an answer. Aware that many search warrants were being issued to uncover the killer, we waited. There was no such thing as patience or understanding at this juncture. We'd suffered the greatest loss. Our son – husband, father, brother, brother-in-law, uncle, cousin, nephew, beloved teacher – had been taken from us. It terrified us that we might never know who did this. There are no words to effectively express our feelings.

The days continued to mount. We were wrenched not only by sorrow, but the realization that the injustice done to all of us might forever leave us questioning. Always looking at every pick-up truck that matched the identity of the one that struck Gavin. Could it be the pick-up adjacent to us at the stoplight? Passing in the other direction? Following behind us? Next to you?

On a warm Friday night, September 21, 2018, we received news that a young man, accompanied by his lawyer, had turned himself in to authorities. Five nights earlier, on Sunday, September 16, an unlicensed 18-year-old driver had left his siblings alone and taken his father's truck to join friends playing beer-pong in an isolated area above a nearby Indian casino. On his way home in the early morning, he hit and killed Gavin. Then, he ran. And hid. By the time he turned himself in, enough time had passed that he was both drug and alcohol free. He showed no remorse, spoke no words of regret. His photo was taken for police records. I gaze into his blank eyes. He confessed to the hit-and-run of Gavin Gladding, posted bail immediately, and was free. Rogelio Alvarez Maravilla didn't see the inside of a jail cell that night, even though he admitted to being the driver of the truck that killed Gavin. Nothing else was said. He just walked away. Gavin *gone.*

The mystery of where Rogelio went or who sheltered him on the day he hit Gavin remains. Who shielded and protected Rogelio while an entire community held its breath waiting to find Gavin's killer? Realistically, we probably will never know for certain. How could we ever begin to forgive if the whodunit remained unsolved? But what we have learned is that his truck was found hidden after being repaired the same morning of the accident. It was found at the home of Rogelio's parents, the home where Rogelio lived. Following an anonymous tip, the CHP found the truck, still filled with pieces of glass covered in Gavin's blood, under a tarp attached to the home Rogelio shared with his family.

Gavin and Susan had an incredible circle of friends we refer to as "The Village." After Gavin's death, this mighty group of 18 showed up each Sunday for weeks to help Susan with whatever she needed around the house. One did the laundry, another cleaned the floors, another washed windows. One particular Sunday I arrived as they were hanging a new chandelier for her in the dining room. Activity everywhere. Love and devotion exhibited by the simplest of tasks. Gavin was loved. His magic endured.

I chose not to see what clothes Gavin was buried in. The task of dressing him fell upon the shoulders of The Village and his Peace Corps buddies, who flew in from all over the world to be with us. They all gathered around us for an entire week after he was killed, and it made sense that they would decide what Gavin would wear on this last day. I have never even asked what clothes they chose to lay him to final rest. I figure it was a T-shirt, shorts, flip-flops, and a cap. I think that is what Gavin would have chosen. That was who Gavin was.

On Monday, September 24, 2018, more than 2,000 mourners attend his funeral. I wear a plain black dress adorned with a beige handknitted scarf Gavin had made for me around my neck. Our family is led into the empty, cavernous church. I focus only on the lonely wooden casket. This box holds my son. As we walk forward, closer to him, I am transfixed to the floor. Approaching the coffin that held my child's body becomes impossible. I simply take my seat.

Our intention was to have an upbeat service to honor an upbeat man. Still, all eyes are drenched with tears. All understand that Gavin is gone. As the hearse carrying Gavin's body to be cremated pulls away from the church, the driver, a friend of Gavin's, blasts out Toto's song "Africa" and other African music. Everyone in the crowd is silent. They understand that this music illustrates an important part of Gavin's life – the Peace Corps. Still weeping, the crowd watches silently, swaying to the music, as the hearse takes Gavin's body away forever.

His body may be gone, but his spirit and remembrances of his special gifs will never die. Or wither away.

Each year on his birthday, we all gather to celebrate him. Year #1 we attended a Mass dedicated to him. Year #2 we gathered in a house at the beach to watch the sunset. Year #3 we held a special dinner honoring the third year of his absence.

Our Christmas tree each year is topped by the "G Love" cap the Village passed out to his many friends. He is our shining star belonging on the top of the tree. The Cabbage Patch doll that was Gavin's is tenderly placed under our tree next to the Nativity scene.

From birth Gavin was nicknamed "Mr. Bunny". As our grandchildren swelled to four in number, I always called them "My Bunnies". Gavin will always be the original Mr. Bunny.

Clovis Roundup, page 1, October 3, 2018

As a tribute to Gavin, his running club tied their shoes to the fence outside Ft. Washington Elementary

More loving messages on the fence outside Ft. Washington Elementary

RITA GLADDING

CHAPTER THREE
DEFINING GAVIN

"His smiles, his high fives, and constant words of encouragement made the campus feel like a safer, warmer place"
The Setareh Tais Family – Ft. Washington Elementary Family
Excerpt from He Loved Us

When Gavin was three years old, we lived on a small cul-de-sac in Houston. I dubbed him Gavin 'Gone' Gladding. By seven o'clock every morning, while Gabrielle (his sister) and I were barely up, watching Mr. Rogers, not even considering breakfast yet, Gavin was already out riding his Big Wheel around the cul-de-sac, rounding up the three next door neighbor children. Gavin was beyond adventuresome. Beyond fearless. He was self-confident from the start and curious, always curious. And completely unafraid to take to the streets alone.

During a visit to Houston from my sister, Paula, and brother-in-law Bob, Gavin was transfixed with his tall uncle (Bob is 6'5"). His height intrigued Gavin. Sitting with Bob in his car, Gavin leaped over the seat from the back of the car, looked up at his uncle, and asked, "Uncle Bob, do you like me?" This was fearless Gavin staring down a man at least three times his size displaying his heart to be received by all.

On one hot, steamy Houston August morning, standing in the kitchen, I turned to see Gavin, who was four at the time, all smiles, holding the most enormous bullfrog I had ever seen. I screamed so loud that he began shaking and crying. But he didn't let go of the frog. In my fit of repugnance, I don't remember taking the frog outside or trying to calm Gavin down. I have since avoided remembering the incident – what kind of mother would scream like that? Years later, remembering the event clearly, Gavin said he never forgot the "frog incident". He would recall the vivid details, giving me a gentle but knowing grin.

Gavin could dress himself when he was three, but his shoelaces were a different story. Ever the problem solver, he quickly learned he could pull on his own Dingo cowboy boots – it was Texas after all – and escape to the outdoors without my help. Along with pictures of his children, Carter and Isla, those cowboy boots are buried with Gavin, next to my childhood rosary, a bottle of holy water from Lourdes, and a T-shirt that Susan added, carrying the slogan, "I tell stupid Dad Jokes". These precious things will be sealed with him for all eternity.

From 1979 - 1983, our family moved around the country quite a bit. From Houston, Texas to St. Louis, Missouri to Columbus, Ohio and finally, Fresno, California. Gary and I were the consummate model of a "retail romance", meeting on an escalator at Foley's, the downtown department store in Houston, where we both worked. It was love at first sight for both of us and marriage followed shortly. Gary spent his entire forty-plus year career in the retail business and always enjoyed the interviewing process. Each interview led to a career promotion, and took us to a different region of our country making new friends as well as experiencing different climates and cultures. Houston had been my home for over twenty years and even though I enjoy new challenges, I was still a bit reluctant to jump across the country. But we found the Midwest very welcoming and each move worked out for the best.

Gavin spent from kindergarten to first grade in three different states and three different schools. He took most of it in his stride, as any five-year-old would. He and Gabrielle (our daughter) readily adapted to three different American cultures – Southern, Midwestern, and, finally, Californian. They both found their own way to acclimate. Gabrielle immediately began to establish friendships that continue today. A group of childhood friends, known as 'The Fresno Girls' shared their tears with Gabrielle, comforting her through our loss. They still get together frequently always continuing to lift each other up.

While Gabrielle was always the more dedicated student, there is no denying that grades two and three were difficult for Gavin. Although he made friends easily, the change of classrooms and teachers with different styles seemed to take a toll on him. For a couple of years he wasn't very enthusiastic about the entire school "thing," he couldn't wait to get home and head outdoors to adventure and explore. His love for the outdoors always trumped everything else. He embraced the humidity, rain, tropical climate in Houston. Both Missouri and Ohio added the element of snow. What child could not love the snow? The afternoon of the Coalinga, California earthquake in 1983, Gavin and his buddy were playing in the corner of our backyard. As I watched the water in the pool begin to lap up over its sides I also heard a low rumble, like a train running underground. All of this was unnoticed by Gavin and his friend, while Gabrielle appeared at the backdoor, sheet white. As she asked me if there had just been an earthquake, I looked across the yard at Gavin playing and said, "Of course not. Your brother didn't move."

Our move to Fresno added to his cadre of favorite things. No matter where we lived, his nature always was to gravitate to the outdoors – and the San Joaquin Valley in Central California was ideal. Gary had grown up in Oakland, California, so accepting a position to return to his home state was exciting. His parents and sister, as well as my only sister, all lived in the Bay Area. It was to become a second homecoming. After the craziness of living in bustling big cities, the entire family fell in love with Fresno in an instant. We left the late April snow still fresh on the ground in Ohio to arrive in sunny Fresno. Fruit, leaves on trees and flowers blooming seemed to put a stamp of approval on our decision to come to California.

We were relieved when by fourth grade Gavin had begun to thrive in school. All students were allowed to compete for "The Block F," starting in grade four. This was the highest honor a student at his school could achieve. Stringent rules were in place, including grade point average, athletic participation, exhibiting outstanding character and leadership traits. As the principal took the podium, he began by saying this award was almost never earned by a 4th grader. He halted his speech as he realized that one 4th grader had achieved the Block F – Gavin Gladding. As his parents, Gary and I never doubted Gavin was special. However, hearing his name called for this prestigious award in an auditorium surrounded by his classmates led to a lump in my throat and a huge smile on my face. Gavin's magic was beginning to shine. He alone, as a fourth grader, had claimed this honor.

Gavin would bound in from school with tales from the day, always cracking us up. Gabrielle was his biggest fan, always encouraging and egging on her little brother's performances. Gathered as a family around the dinner table, Gavin was first to share the experiences of the day. His stories were always the best. He wore both his heart and his soul on his sleeve. One day in fifth grade, he reported that his entire class was measured for height and that there were only two people shorter than him in his class: Alison and Mandy. We worried that being small might be awkward, but Gavin never dwelled on his height. Entering 9th grade, he and his sister were finally back together on the same campus. Gabrielle came home from their first day of school, looked t me with a solemn face and said, "Mom, Gavin is really short." I shot her a warning glance. As a family, we could all see how small Gavin was, but never made it seem important. Gabrielle added, "No, Mom, I saw him standing with a group of his friends. He is really small."

The Gladding men grew late. Gary had graduated from high school standing 5'10" and by the time he finished college, he towered at 6'2". We won't mention that I carry short, Italian genes along with my 47 first cousins. During the summer between Gavin's junior and senior year, he grew so much that we scheduled many appointments with an orthopedic surgeon due to Gavin's complaints of pain in his right knee. He and I were both stunned when the doctor informed us that, at sixteen, his growth plate was wide open. He had an unknown number of inches of growth still to come. Returning to the volleyball court in the spring of his senior year, the other parents began to ask us if we had watered him with Miracle Grow. He was over six feet tall.

Always moving forward, always thinking ahead, Gavin was only in the 7th grade when he announced that he intended to attend the University of California, Santa Barbara to study about the earth and environment, then live on the land. Academics came easily to him. Especially science and math, although neither were his priority. Gavin knew how difficult it was to be admitted to University of California Santa Barbara, so he worked hard.

Then again, his athletic endeavors were also extremely important to him and presented more of a struggle, due to his small stature until his senior year. Soccer and volleyball were his chosen sports in high school. As a freshman, the volleyball team used to throw him from person to person for entertainment. But he never gave up. We held our breath, said a few prayers, hoping that he would make the varsity volleyball team as a senior. Gavin was ready to accept the coach's decision. Our kitchen phone attached to the wall in those days rang the morning the coach posted the squad members. Gavin had made the team. He was ecstatic. We were relieved. I received this text on Monday, September 17, 2018, the day after Gavin was killed: *"Dear Rita, I was so horribly saddened to hear the news about Gavin. My heartfelt condolences to you and the entire family. I adored your son, and always will. Please let me know if I can help with anything or I can support the family in any way. All of my love, Coach Roy."* Roy came to Gavin's service carrying a picture of Bullard High School's Valley Championship Volleyball team to present to Carter (Gavin's son). Carter accepted the photo with a smile filled with pride on his face.

His volleyball teammates were his best buddies. Friday nights, one of them would swing by, pick him up, and I know little else! After school, Gavin headed anywhere outside on his bike. Most afternoons he spent working out or playing tennis at our neighborhood club. Fishing with his father or trekking with his sister, he was never happier. His favorite weekends were spent with family or friends at either Huntington Lake or Bass Lake. Outdoors, in the wilderness, exploring, these were still the things he treasured most, ever since he learned to dress himself at three.

Always true to his word, Gavin did indeed attend UCSB, graduating with a Bachelor of Science in Environmental Science. When preparing to leave Fresno, he refused the gift of a new bike, opting for his old Junker. We were appalled until he told us what went on at that campus. There was a practice of 'trading' bikes to get to classes. All students arrived for classes with one bike and just left with another. We were horrified, but Gavin assured us that he wasn't a thief. He participated in interfraternity volleyball games. Played tennis with my first cousin, Victor, who lived in Santa Barbara. Gavin declined a few invitations to go 'bar-hopping' with Victor saying he got plenty of partying in at school. He pledged Sigma Chi fraternity his first semester. The first visit Gary and I made to his fraternity house prompted me to ask him: "Do you know what dysentery is?" When he answered, "No," I explained that I wouldn't describe the illness, but that I was sure he would have it by the end of the semester. He didn't contract dysentery until his Peace Corps days, thank God. He went on to hold several offices in the Sigma Chi fraternity.

Gavin loved college. Living on the beach of the Pacific Ocean was special to him. His fraternity brothers recognized immediately his innate ability to lead, to remain level-headed, to be there for each of them. As President of Sigma Chi, he enjoyed the role. His sense of humor was always a part of conversations we had with his frat brothers. He was known to entice them to take a short hike that ended up being miles long. When I visited his fraternity house during his senior year, his room was freezing cold. I asked if he could shut the window. With a wry look on his face, he explained that someone had fallen out of his window (on the first floor) and it contained no glass. Later, Gary received a phone call from Gavin explaining he had broken the window and the bill to repair it was on the way.

Another excellent example of his unique humor was when I would ask him to call home on Sunday evening, as soon as he returned driving from Fresno back to Santa Barbara, to let me know he was safe. The phone would ring on Tuesday. Gavin always said the same thing, "The traffic was horrible."

Late in his senior year of college, Gavin called home to announce that he had joined the Peace Corps. Stunned, I replied, "They can't take you that quickly!" He confirmed with a laugh that they could, and they did. Another promise kept. As a child of the 60's, I knew about John Kennedy's program to improve the entire world. Gavin had the same plan. On July 2, 1998, Gary and I accompanied Gavin to the Fresno Air Terminal to send him off to the Peace Corps. All three of us were trying to be brave. We hugged, watched him walk across the tarmac, climb the steps to the plane to depart. At the top of the stairs, Gavin stopped, turned and waved to us. He had no idea if we were still there watching, but that final gesture of love, exposing his soul by a simple wave, sent Gary and me into deep sobs. That was an example of Gavin's mystic, always making sure we understood how much he cared for us.

Gavin served his Peace Corps tour in The Gambia, West Africa. The third poorest country on the African continent, geographically it is known as "the smile on the Atlantic coast of Africa." The Gambia River forms the smile. Gavin was assigned to stay in the village of Charmen, across the river from Banjul, The Gambia's capitol. He was issued his own mud hut with thatched roof along with a ten-pound bag of cement to be used to line the private latrine that he dug himself. In The Gambia, three different dialects were spoken: Mandinka, Wolof and Fula. Gavin's village, Charmen, spoke Wolof. Gavin immediately began immersing himself in their native language by following the little kids around the village learning the names of things in their native tongue. It was then that he was given the name Abdoulraxman. When he was told that the meaning of his name was "Messenger from God," he took it humbly in his pace. Never questioning, just accepting. He used this foreboding moniker as his email address for years. Out of the 39 graduates that composed his Peace Corps class, Gavin was chosen to make a video to promote their volunteerism. Unfortunately, that video has gone missing.

The Gambia is where Gavin's life as an educator began. In a mud hut with nothing but a dirt floor, working with children who had a limited grasp of the English language, Gavin became completely at ease teaching the children in his village. This was the commencement of Gavin's special skills as a teacher. He ultimately was able to touch many students on two continents. His confidence in his role as teacher was apparent from the beginning. Whether he was sharing his innate ability to speak extemporaneously or when working from a written lesson plan, the desire to become an educator began growing within him. The message he shared ignited others to immerse themselves in education. More of Gavin's charisma.

When Gavin returned home from The Gambia, he found things changed in his native country in the two-plus years he was volunteering. The best example was when I asked him to please take my car out of the garage and handed him the keyless fob. He looked at me quizzically and asked where the key was?

The first family event we attended upon Gavin's return was my Godson Chris' wedding. Gavin was a groomsman standing proudly behind his cousin. At the reception, he was introduced to a good friend of Chris' who was a high school history teacher. Mike was intrigued by the fact that Gavin had just returned from Africa. After a brief conversation, he suggested to Gavin, "Hey, why don't you come and tell my class about what the experience was like?" And Gavin did. He thoroughly enjoyed being back in the classroom. According to their teacher, Mike, his students were fascinated with the presentation. More enchantment.

Gavin decided to take the California Basic Educational Skills test to begin substitute teaching. His teaching experiences in The Gambia had been an unexpected turning point in his life. His love of teaching children resurfaced upon his return home and Gavin knew this was how he wanted to spend the rest of his life. In his pursuit to find a job once back in the USA, Gavin kept a close eye on the Peace Corps website for returning volunteers. Bingo. A listing from Blue Ridge Outdoor Educational Center in Toccoa, Georgia caught his attention. "Experimental Environmental Education" was listed beneath its logo. Blue Ridge Outdoor Educational Center was an environmental camp for high school students from the Atlanta school system.

Interviewing over the phone, Gavin was offered the position. He spent two years in Georgia working with students and living on the land. By his second year, he was promoted to head of the center. Gary and I were overwhelmed by Georgia's beauty during our two visits to the camp.

My quest, as the eternal Italian mother, was to figure out a way to entice Gavin to return to Fresno, to have both of my children as nearby as possible. I scoured the paper for articles involving the San Joaquin River Parkway and Conservation Trust, Inc. This is our river that runs on the northern border of Fresno. I forwarded articles on to Georgia: The salmon are running upstream again; Eagles have been sighted above the camp; River Camp is back in session for the summer at Scout Island. Finally, after many months, Gavin called to ask for details about this organization. In 2003, he was ready to come home. The interviewing process was over the phone. It worked. My prayers had been answered. Our boy was returning home to Fresno and bringing the love of his life, Susan, with him. To stay.

Gavin met Susan while both were working in Atlanta, Georgia during the summer of 2001. Gavin was walking the Georgia Pipeline with two coworkers when they asked him if he had met Susan, from the office. Gavin answered no. Both men replied, "You are going to love Susan." I received a call from Gavin in August, 2001. Repeating the story to me, he ended with, "And Mom, I love Susan." I asked him what he loved most. "Her smile" was his answer.

The first time I met Susan, I easily was able to agree that her smile was exceptional. Warm, welcoming, loving. Susan, a Pennsylvanian, was first introduced to Fresno when she attended Gabrielle's marriage to Garrett Ruby on December 28, 2001. It was a beautiful event with a reception held at the Fresno Museum of Art and Science before it closed forever in 2009. Gavin was so proud to show Susan that besides being surrounded by mountains and a gorgeous river, our city had an accredited museum. Back to his old stomping grounds, Gavin took Susan up every trail and down every hill he had explored as a child.

Gavin first joined the River Parkway as River Steward Coordinator. He went on to become Outdoor Activities Program Manager, then the River Camp Director. He remained as Director of Special Programs for the River Parkway Trust from 2011 – 2015. Initially hired to stamp out a vicious weed that was taking over the natural habitat of our river, Gavin's personality, ease with others, and natural ability to become a trailblazer became apparent. He loved every job he did for the Parkway and the staff loved him right back. Those first years back in Fresno were extraordinary for the entire family.

Gabrielle and her family, husband Garrett, biological son, Jett and their adopted angel, Finley, were delighted when Gavin and Susan purchased their dream home on the same street where they lived. 'Uncle G' and 'Sue-Soon' were raising their two children six houses away from their cousins. A mother's dream come true – seeing her grown children remain so close. Their bond goes back to infancy. The night Gabrielle went into labor with Jett, it was Gavin she woke up to sit with her. As her labor pains grew closer and closer together, Gavin was timing them as the rest of us slept. Born three weeks early, Gavin was the first of our entire family to hold his nephew, Jett. It was a blissful time. Unable to become pregnant a second time, Gab and Garrett were blessed to adopt a baby girl, Finley. As the perfect addition to our family, gatherings became more prevalent. Gavin, master of the bar-b-que, became the family chef. After Gavin passed we never had another family bar-b-que. We gave the grill away and never replaced it.

Gavin treasured each day he spent serving in the outdoors, improving our river and becoming part of the Parkway community. His magic touched hundreds of children, ages four thru 16. Again, he was given a name by his students. Always in charge, Gavin became known as the "Jefe" for the four years he was at the helm of River Camp. The campers thought this to be the best name for him – he was the chief. To this day, I run into people in the grocery store who tell tales of their child's days at River Camp with the "Jefe." Instead of crying, now I smile. Cherished memories remain.

Parenthood comes without a manual. After many months of prayer and anticipation a marvelous, perfect child appears. Out into the world they go, and you wonder, *what is going to happen? Can Gary and I provide the home for our children I always dreamed of?* Like a miracle unfolding before our eyes, our family grew to the number of four. Always wanting that third child, I was told by four different obstetricians in four different states that I couldn't carry another baby. It just wasn't going to happen. So, the four Gladding's went forward.

My Italian heritage, along with Gary's English, Polish, and German background, ended up being a divine combination. We did our best to always sit down to dinner, play games, and take bike rides together. Praying that we laid a good foundation, both of our children became impressive parents, each in their own way. Gabrielle devoted hours to her children providing different activities to strengthen their minds and body every day. As a sophomore in high school, Jett earned a scholarship to play baseball for Fresno State University. Finley, our adopted angel, became the first Buchanan freshman in the history of the school to letter in a sport – gymnastics.

Gavin and Susan also set up a warm, nurturing environment for their children, Carter and Isla. Susan had the wonderful opportunity to work from home, while Gavin was loving his outdoor work with the Parkway. During his last years running River Camp, he took both kids along. This was a perfect opportunity for the two nature-loving children. Then came the summer when Gavin was no longer running the camp. Even after he left the Parkway, the kids always spent at least two weeks enjoying the outside. Gavin instilled in them the love of the outdoors that both he and Susan shared. Instead of teaching summer school, for which the additional money would certainly have been useful, Gavin chose to stay home with his children all summer. Susan needed the peace to do her job. He made the summer days charmed for his two "kiddos," as he referred to them. The deal Gavin struck with his children was so "Gavin." The arrangement was that they gave him until 11 o'clock each morning to finish whatever chores he needed to do, and then he was all theirs. Every day was a different adventure. Canoeing on the river, camping, spending time at our condo at Huntington Lake, fishing, doing puzzles, exploring. Always outdoors. He was theirs alone from 11 in the morning until 5:00 p.m. every day. He made every minute of every day extraordinary. The last summer Gavin shared with his children before his senseless death was when they were eight and ten. A life lost to a drunken driver. Fairy-tale summers ended. Gavin *gone.*

I saved many of the correspondences Gavin sent out during his years with the Parkway. While serving as River Stewards Coordinator, Gavin wrote numerous appeal letters asking for volunteers to help clean up the banks of the San Joaquin. I could feel his spirit shining through every word. Searching, always searching to improve our world, this excerpt from one such letter is a plea to better our community, to better our world.

A Call for Arms

How much of a difference can one person really make? Two legs, two arms, two hands, one mind, one heart. What is the power of one in a world where one in a million is rapidly transitioning to one in a billion? One person cannot move a mountain; eliminate a prolific noxious weed; or clean up a dirty river.

In an individual lies the ability to inspire, inform, and bring hope to others. Hope that one day our river will not be perceived as a large flowing garbage dump. Hope that we can impede the progress of exotic plants bent on total dominance of our native habitat. Hope that one day we will be able to take a slow stroll along the river on a Parkway path.

The only way that these hopes are going to be realized is with the help of each one of us individually. By talking to those that surround us and increasing the awareness of the River Parkway Trust, its mission, and its activities along the river we can bring about change. We can inspire people to take action.

In another appeal letter, Gavin included a quote from the environmentalist Aldo Leopold: "...perhaps our grandsons, having never seen a wild river, will miss the chance to set a canoe in singing waters...glad I shall never be young without a wild country to be young in."

Gavin wrote continual letters of appeal during his time as River Stewards Coordinator. One of my favorites describes a cold day in February:

Oh, the wind and the rain. The most amazing thunderstorm passed over us yesterday giving us nature's version of pyrotechnic laser light show. Breaking bolts of lightning giving way to a crisp thundercrack always start my heart racing. The patient seeds of last fall are receiving what they needed from the storms...moisture. The banks of the river are awash with a luscious flowing green of new growth reaching its way towards the sun. What a glorious time to enjoy both the beauty and tranquility of the San Joaquin!

In another appeal, Gavin included this quote by Margaret Meade: "Never doubt that a small group of committed citizens can change the world. Indeed, it is the only thing that ever has."

Gavin loved his time at the Parkway, but he continued to be pulled by a strong desire to be a classroom teacher. He attended night classes at Fresno State to receive his teaching credential while still working full time for the Parkway. His student teaching experience was at Buchanan High School. Offered a position to stay there, Gavin chose to begin his career at Alta Sierra Junior High School.

Although Gavin was first and foremost a son, husband, father, and uncle, he was also an extraordinary educator. I remember his tales from the trenches of teaching middle school, much like the funny after-school stories he entertained us with as a child. Frequently, he took Oscar, his dog, with him. Our family joke was that Oscar weighed more than I did, but Oscar's temperament was the same as Gavin's – mellow. The kids loved this big black Labradoodle joining them for class. Many years later we learned Gavin was referred to by the girls as 'the prince'!

He began influencing seventh grade students in General Science before agreeing to become the Advanced Placement Environmental Science teacher at Clovis West High School. Each year his junior year APES students participated in the state Science Olympiad competition. His students knew he would go above and beyond to give them any assistance they needed. Gavin's classes always filled to maximum capacity. "Mr. G's APES" was the class everyone wanted to be part of. His reputation as an invigorating, engaging teacher spread fast. He loved his subject, his students, his job. From agreeing to become the volleyball coach at Alta Sierra, to teaching Advanced Placement

Environmental Science at Clovis West High School, to participating in the Science Olympiad competition each year, he was always there. The year after he was killed, these high school students, at a school he had left two years before, made T-shirts for the 2019 Olympiad with "Gold for Gladding" written on each shirt. His magic wasn't forgotten.

Gavin was encouraged by co-workers and administrative staff members at Clovis West High School to attend a special program at Fresno State University to earn his master's degree in school administration. His colleagues were clearly aware of his abilities and his gift for teaching. He had a job offer to advance to Guidance Instructor Specialist/Vice Principal even before he finished his studies. His role included greeting each student every morning at Fort Washington Elementary School. He knew their names; he was there for each of them. Respected. Loved. Available to both students and fellow teachers, he performed the role of Vice-Principal, which included disciplinarian, with an easy, poised style. It was while serving as a Vice Principal that his life was taken by a drunk driver.

Gavin's original Dingo boots, circa 1978

Gavin and Oscar

CHAPTER FOUR
EIGHT MONTHS IN THE COUNTY COURTHOUSE

"But above all, Mr. Gladding was a great man; a great man that deserved so much better." Ariana – Student from Clovis West High School
Excerpt from He Loved Us

To completely understand the contextual background to Gavin's death, particulars are necessary. Through these details our course of action to honor Gavin's life evolves. To provide succinct information recounting each court case are, unfortunately, essential.

The background follows:

There were three individuals involved in Gavin's hit-and-run death and its cover-up. From October, 2018, through May 2019, we were to face five court appearances at the Fresno County Courthouse.

Our plight to seek justice for Gavin began on October 26, 2018, when the admitted driver of the truck that mowed Gavin down pled "No Contest" to the felony charge of fleeing an accident. Also added to the felony charge were three misdemeanors: vehicular manslaughter, driving without a license and destroying evidence. The fine for driving without a California driver's license was forty dollars.

The definition of a No Contest plea in California is that the accused accepts conviction but avoids a factual admission of guilt. The driver who left him on the side of the road without knowing if he was alive or dead, was handcuffed right in front of us and taken to jail. His plea of No Contest made the entire courtroom proceedings agonizing. On the night Rogelio came out of hiding, he admitted to hitting Gavin, but the ability to plead No Contest would ensure that he could be convicted of the felony without standing trial, without the certainty of prison time.

As Rogelio was handcuffed standing three feet from us, the judge confined him to jail. He was to return in a month for sentencing. Rogelio Maravilla, never looked at us. To my eyes he never showed one ounce of emotion. Our slight ray of satisfaction was that he might receive the maximum sentence of four years in prison. We prayed for justice. That morning we openly wept with hope in the courtroom.

By the time Rogelio made his final court appearance in November, 2018, the judge handling his case had received more than 200 letters in support of giving Rogelio a full four-year sentence. According to California law, the sentence would be the judge's choice. Amongst the letters was one written by my 12-year-old granddaughter, Finley Sarah Ruby: "Uncle G was a great man. He taught me to fish, how to ride my bike, how to pick up his dog's poop, how to understand math and science, and how to be kind like him. The man that hit Uncle G deserves to be held in jail because he killed an innocent, kind person who didn't deserve this." The other approximately 199 letters carried the same sentiment. Apparently, the weight of these statements didn't resonate with the judge.

In the courtroom on Monday, November 26, 2018, Gary spoke first. He is a tall man and an accomplished speaker. He is strong. His voice is stern.

forthcoming and honest. He led the charge we all would follow by simply asking for the maximum sentence.

With Gary standing at my side, I addressed the court for the first time. I wasn't scared. I wasn't apprehensive about what I was about to say. I was angry, but I knew that controlling my anger was essential. I tried to remain unemotional, but my child was dead. My pain was still raw. What was I doing standing in front of a judge pleading with him to deliver the maximum sentence? Harsh as this was to admit, the only hope I had left was to convey to our first judge how I felt about the unjustness of the entire process. Only one person had control over the sentence – the judge seated on the bench. He needed to grasp this message. My Gavin, Abdoulraxman, had sent this message.

"Gavin was my son. As a mother I sought many things for both my children. Never did I imagine I would be seeking justice for a life that was ended way too soon."

Gabrielle followed me, pleading for the same maximum sentence. My 15-year-old grandson, Jett Sullivan Ruby, was next: "On the day Uncle G was hit and killed, I was the one who watched his kids while everyone was in the hospital. The vivid memory of my two little cousins – eight and ten – crying in my arms, asking if their dad will be okay, still haunts me. Seeing them lost of hope and broken in spirit was the most chilling and real experience I've ever had. Please give the maximum sentence you can."

Susan was last. Gabrielle stood by her side during her testimony, as she tearfully spoke of the terrible loss Rogelio Maravilla had caused her and her two young children, Carter, ten, and Isla, eight. She also pleaded for the most stringent sentence. The judge listened patiently. The courtroom was absolutely silent.

For the defense, an Assistant Pastor at St. Jude Catholic Church, Easton, CA., offered condolences to our Gladding family. He added that he "had spoken with Maravilla several times and found him remorseful." But he, too, was baffled as to why he didn't stop to help Gavin. "I don't know what possessed him to leave the scene. He may not have known how serious it was, at least that is what he told me." More necessary background: apparently, Rogelio never told his Priest that he and the two others returned to the scene of the crime twice that morning, to ensure that no evidence that could convict them remained.

As a cradle Catholic and Extraordinary Minister of Holy Communion at St. Anthony of Padua Catholic Church in Fresno, I found it impossible to understand what this holy man said to the court that day. I wanted to know if Rogelio had requested and received the sacrament of reconciliation. I wanted to remind the Priest that Rogelio demonstrated lack of judgement that morning by fleeing the scene. I wanted this Priest to explain why his parishioner seemed incapable of knowing right from wrong.

How could I live the rest of my life with this numbing belief? This was the first moment I realized forgiveness would also be part of the footpath necessary to mend. Healing became so much more important than grieving. To rebuild, we must be willing to pardon what had happened. Or recognize that we would carry this burden for the rest of our lives. To survive this tragedy, to believe a true accident had occurred, we must allow our inner strength to surface.

Our strength must reflect what we all believe Gavin would have wished for: accountability and forgiveness. The portion of this story that wasn't printed anywhere were the words used in summation by the three different judges we faced. The reality that we were denied what we had asked from each judge – full four-year sentences – had stupefied us all. Even though all three defendants had become convicted felons, these light sentences still seemed irrational to our family. To keep our souls from festering, with pain still in our hearts, we know how to go forward to survive. Could we alter this leniency to avoid this misery being inflicted on other families? I believe the entire family knew, at that moment, we would have to try. Drawing from deep within ourselves, we absorb the reality of the necessity for compassion to serve others.

In Rogelio's case, the judge added statements such as, "The defendant was able to wipe out cell phone records from the iCloud. The defendant and other two involved in the hit-and-run crime involving Gavin returned to the scene two more times that morning trying to remove any evidence against them that the CHP might have missed...that's unusual," the judge said, quizzically. Then, his next words shocked us. "But he is young and this is his first offense." My heart began to race. To me, this was inarguably, most assuredly, an easy maximum sentence to deliver. What more evidence was needed? A man was hit and left to die on the side of the road. Criminals returning to the scene of the crime to cover their tracks? A severely damaged pick-up truck that was repaired in less than six hours. An unlicensed driver who was hidden for five days to be sure all traces of drugs and alcohol were gone from his system. Then the judgment: Rogelio's sentence was to be just three years.

Rogelio stared forward the entire time the judge was sentencing him, standing up stick straight. No movement, no visible emotion was displayed. To me, he appeared to show no regret. I kept searching his face beginning to understand that, for my own sanity, forgiveness would be necessary. Gavin *gone.*

Rogelio was released from prison 13 months later. He was home for Christmas 2019...but Gavin will never be home for Christmas again. Dumbfounded, I continue to wonder why Gavin's life wasn't worth more than a prison sentence of 13 months. Our direction became clear – with tolerance and compassion, we would attempt to change a California law.

When the judge sentenced him to a prison term, an unidentified woman screamed, "My, baby! My baby!" as Rogelio Maravilla was taken from the courtroom. And we began to wonder, who was the victim here? Gavin or Rogelio? And the sentence? Three years, not four. Astonished, again we wept. The Fresno Bee front page headline on November 27, 2018 read, "Fresno Teen Given Three Years in Hit-and-Run Killing of Vice Principal."

Many loving and loyal friends accompanied us each time we were summoned to appear at the courthouse. Close friends were there the day Rogelio received his lenient sentence. The woman sitting next to our dear friends exclaimed to them, "Why is he going to jail? He's not a criminal." My friend turned to her and said, "No. He is a murderer."

The female passenger in the car, Fernanda Lopez, had retained a lawyer who from November 2018 through May 2019 kept asking for a continuance. He needed more time. Was she going to plead something other than No Contest as her boyfriend, now a convicted felon, had done? The uncertainty of her plea kept our minds and hearts racing for months.

The third person involved was Moises Guerero. He was summoned by Rogelio and Fernanda immediately after the hit-and-run to cover up the crime, to fix the car and help hide it. More background: another plea of No

58

Contest rings out in the courtroom on March 5, 2019. As Moises was to face sentencing the verdict given was the same to us as Rogelio's - unbelievable. His judge convicted him of the felony of aiding and abetting in a hit-and-run. He then gave him a stern lecture. The judge warned him, "If you are ever in front of me again, I promise I will charge you with murder." I covered my mouth to keep from shouting in skepticism. No jail time at all. He walked out of the courtroom right in front of us. With so much leniency given, again we began to wonder who the victim was here. Not Gavin, but the defendants? Our actions going forward again were focused on preventing this same scenario to play out for any other family. I kept hearing the word *forgive* ringing in my head.

As we gathered ourselves together after this second lenient verdict to walk out of the courtroom, we were summoned by the court reporter to come forward to meet her. We approached the partition where she was waiting. With tears in her eyes and a breaking voice she tells us, "My two granddaughters went to Fort Washington. They cried for two days after Mr. Gladding was killed. They loved him."

While awaiting her trial, Fernanda Lopez requested to be free to continue with her life as if nothing had happened and three different judges granted her request. In April, her lawyer suggested the judge allow her to finish her semester at Fresno State University. Her wish was granted. To this moment I remember covering my mouth with my hand to smother the scream escaping from my throat. Our family and lives were being destroyed and she got to finish her semester at Fresno State. Who was the victim? We were living a daily nightmare. Each day required monumental strength to continue. Prayers and our convictions must triumph.

Finally, on May 15, 2019, Fernanda, the passenger, pled No Contest, as the others had. My question to the judge was, "Your Honor, if you let Ms. Lopez walk out of this courtroom, you alone will have to answer the question: What would I be doing if it were my son that was mowed down by these two people and left to die... DIE...on the side of Friant Road?" We received no verbal answer. Though I felt the judge had looked at me with understanding, the proceedings were allowed to continue.

Our family was now readying for the third defendant to be sentenced. Fernanda was convicted of a felony for aiding and abetting in a hit-and-run and several misdemeanors for concealing evidence in a hit-and-run and leaving the scene. The entire courtroom was taken aback as she was handcuffed and sentenced to eight months in Fresno County jail. There had been suggestions that she would serve no time at all. Dressed in an off-the-shoulder blouse paired with tight slacks, a weak apology to us slips out of Fernanda's mouth. I could see a single tear running down her cheek as she was hand cuffed and led away a few feet in front of us. I wanted to stand, grab her, shake her. Powerless to make any changes to her moderate sentence, I fell forward in my seat, held my daughter's hand and silently wept. We had to find the strength and courage to end this.

Yet again, like her two accomplices, Fernanda never looked at us. She was released four months later, in August, free to continue her life. Her judge suggested in the future she could address high school students about the dangers she had faced using misjudgment and being involved in a hit-and-run He neglected to add that she and Rogelio never stopped to render aid, that they sped away, leaving Gavin alive on the side of the road. Fernanda was also placed on three years of probation. She was free just months later, far sooner than if she had been given the maximum sentence. It was as if Gavin's right died with him. We didn't realize that the driver and accomplices had more rights than our son who died. A very hard reality to swallow. Our hands were tied for the moment.

Grief displays itself in many forms. It changes shape but never ends. After the death of your child comes the initial shock. The shrieking. The shouting with eyes lifted to Heaven, and the sobbing long before the reality sets in. And it isn't pretty. You are hugged by seemingly hundreds of people. You try to hug back, try to speak, try to stop crying. You pray grief will evolve, but somehow know it will never diminish.

We pray for closure, but don't feel it. Each journey to court to hear the sentencing was almost like experiencing his death all over again. We would have to find another way to hope for justice. Alexander Dumas wrote these words included in The Count of Monte Christo nearly one and a half centuries ago. They are descriptive of how we feel today. "The heart breaks when it has swelled too much in the warm breath of hope, then finds itself enclosed in cold reality."

In this written account, and when addressing the court, I used hard terms when describing Rogelio. Not once in any courtroom did the judges or anyone else use those explicit, descriptive words. I use these harsh words because I believe that Rogelio and Fernanda possess free will, as we all do. It was their choice to drive drunk or drugged, and it was their choice to flee. I'd rather believe Rogelio to have been completely intoxicated, beyond all reason and thought, than believe that he was afraid to face the penalty for killing a man. My belief in the goodness of every human being just won't let me accept that he was sober minded when left my son to die.

This has been the hardest piece of this story for me to write. My stomach continues to roil. I still want to throw up. My forgiveness slowly surfaces. I believe Gavin would have also pleaded for fairness for himself, but ultimately he would have forgiven them for their actions. That was Gavin. Plainly, this was a part of the message God intended him to share.

We were a family broken, but never deterred. We will forever battle to change these inadequate punishments for taking an innocent man's life. We could not just stand by and watch this unacceptable scene continue to play out. Two innocent children have been cheated of spending their lives with a loving father.

In December 2019, after serving 13 months, Rogelio was freed. The two accomplices, Moises and Fernanda, even though both were also convicted of felony crimes, had managed to continue their lives for months before any strict rulings were made. Of the accomplices, only Fernanda wound up serving time in the county jail. The justice we prayed for never came. Thus, the reality of the court system in the state we live in became clear to us. Justice, as we had longed perceived it, was not to happen. It would be up to us to make something happen.

Soon after his death, we began to build a non-profit in Gavin's name, to honor his love for working outdoors in the environment. We received approval for the Gavin Gladding Foundation in record time. Funds raised would be used to send students studying the sciences to higher learning platforms and, of course, to support the River Parkway Trust by funding River Camp.

Currently, we are awarding scholarships to students from Clovis West High School only. A major goal toward making Gavin's life unforgettable will be to be able to do the same for all the Clovis Unified School District high schools to receive scholarships provided by Gavin's foundation. This is a message we received from Abdoulraxman.

Abdoulraxman "Messenger from God"

CHAPTER FIVE
SEEKING JUSTICE

"Mr. Gladding was a one-of-a-kind individual. So many people can say how he had such an impact on their life as an educator, but he just made a difference to us all as a human being". Katie – Student at Clovis West High School
Excerpt from He Loved Us

After the three lenient sentences were handed down, our determination to assist other families grew even stronger. Our family would fight for change in California through the legislative system. This was crystal clear. Change the penalty for felony hit-and-run. We would get it done no matter how many times we had to try. It became a passion, a passion to assist the residents of the state of California. Passion for justice for my son. Passion necessary to live, passion to cope with the pain and continue forward.

Our bill was simple. We sought to increase the sentence for Felony Hit-and-Run from the current punishment of two to four years in prison to four to six years instead. Assemblyman Jim Patterson walked us through each step along the way. Even this slight increase, though not commensurate with the hit-and-run crime, would provide an ounce of justice for Gavin. Present day and night, the compulsion to pass Gavin's Law began to exhaust me. Fighting to keep forgiveness at the forefront was challenging. Every thought fleeting or not, became a part of my every breath. Nights were the worst. Silent and still, my shouts escape, propelling me forward to face each new day to continue our plight. A plight that contained forgiveness. A message

Abdoulraxman was sending.

I know I will awake needing the energy necessary to propel our plan to alter a law every day. Although I am always on the verge of tears, I manage to smile. Frequent visits with Monsignor Rob seem to flush out feelings that I somehow keep in check. My anger surfaces whenever I talk about the extreme loss the world has suffered. And the anger actually helps with my broken heart. Strange to reflect on what was happening to me as an *activity*. My therapy is provided by numerous friends always consoling me, joining me in tears on the rare occasions I can't hold them back. Gavin *gone.*

I admire Gary's ability to cope with our loss. Hanging in his office is the huge photograph of Gavin from the funeral. I stare down at the floor each time I walk down the hallway passing this room. Even a glimpse of Gavin's larger than life image sends me spinning. Gary claims the picture brings him peace. He communicates with Gavin by continuing to look at his picture. Another message from son to father.

Initially, the district attorney assigned to Gavin's case told us the man who caused the death of our son would probably not serve any time at all for his crime. When my daughter-in-law, Susan, heard this, she gasped. Susan tells us later, "I almost fell off my chair." This man had robbed her of a husband, her children of their father. At that moment we began to realize we would be facing a tough journey. There had to be some sort of equality somewhere. Abhorrent acts such as Gavin's death had to be accounted for. His life was worth more than a maximum sentence of four years. Despite everything we faced, could we manage to modify a law? Our goal was established.

Our pathway to justice became politically convoluted and not really a pathway at all. It was more like charging into a chaotic battlefield or tearing down a multi-lane freeway in the wrong direction facing the oncoming traffic, sirens screaming as loudly as we were. All the time we refused to admit we could be facing an endless road trip with no off-ramp in sight. We were determined not to become a lost cause. Committed to continue making every effort to fight to accomplish our goal, we stood our ground. We would only go headfirst to succeed. To help others.

CHAPTER SIX
BATTLING FOR GAVIN'S LAW

"We can all strive to live more like Mr. Gladding. An amazing teacher but an even more amazing human being with an incredible faith and heart."
Abby and Kate – Students/sisters at Clovis West High School
Excerpt from He Loved Us

Choices, choices, choices. I become paralyzed with indecision. I pray harder for the miracle of his return. I get up and go, always moving frontward, but somehow, I never get ahead. I try to be strong for our daughter, Gabrielle, now our only child, who has suffered her grief so bravely. I pray for our daughter-in-law, I pray for our grandchildren. In the immediate days after Gavin's death, I receive many calls from my sister, Paula, Gabrielle's Godmother, who was vacationing in Ireland when Gavin died. Our calls were filled with screaming and sobbing. The same is true of Gary's sister, Lorrie. Calls from my cousin Patti, Gavin's Godmother, vacationing in Greece caused more tears. I'm clear that the hollowness of my misery cannot rule my life. Blinded by the unhappiness, I still recognize that dedication is always the answer. Circumstances became absolutely impossible for us not to accept that God was clearly defining our course. A message was sent. Abdoulraxman, the Messenger from God, had sent word: help others.

There is a glaring loophole in state law that actually benefits drunken drivers who leave the scene of an accident. Drunk, or otherwise impaired drivers, who leave the scene and sober up before their arrest, can avoid the 15-year maximum sentence for a felony DUI conviction. A four-year sentence is the most they will face. At a time when we were still experiencing fresh raw misery, an obsession grows. Still numb, we clearly knew that to make a difference we would have to work within the system and do it ourselves. We would seek establishment of justice for other families who would not, in the future, be made to suffer through the same dreadful tragedy we had. Our love for others surfaced. Our need to come to the aid of other grief-stricken families stood out clearly. A new law to effect hit-and-run drivers must be written and my family was the one to do just that. Attempting to buck the California legislative system started our journey to recovery. Our family's avenue to rebuilding would become the fight we would take up with the State of California in Gavin's name.

Assembly Bill 582, "Gavin's Law" became our goal. Our motto was "close the loophole." Hit and run drivers are self-admitted slayers who are rewarded by leaving the scene at the time of the accident. California law today states that drivers under the influence, when caught at the scene of the accident, be charged with vehicular manslaughter, and sentenced from four to ten years, or more. However, the driver receives a lesser penalty if they flee the scene, show up a few days later, sober and protected by an attorney. This loophole incentivizes drivers to flee especially if drugs or alcohol were involved. The sentencing of prison time for hit-and-run penalties is much less than for manslaughter. The need for Gavin's Law couldn't be clearer to us, but could we sway the four committees in both houses, plus the Assembly floor, the Senate floor and then the Governor of California to understand how particularly heinous this lenient sentence was? It becomes apparent that many committee members had not been properly prepared for what our bill was trying to achieve. After our testimony, committee members hovered around the chairperson to try to get the story straight.

Breathless with anticipation, we listened as the committee chairman began to address the crowd. Rather than vote, the Committee Chairman stood to address the chamber. We listened in some state between shock and reality to him grant this committee the opportunity to bring Gavin's Law back after further discussion. In disbelief, filled with joy, we left to spend the next eight months preparing our return to Sacramento.

Emotionally drained, we piled back in the car after the proceedings, heading home, thankful and knowing we would be going back soon to make our case. Feeling as if we were swimming in the deep end of the pool and nearly drowning in our unhappiness, our mission to create a solution to the problem, and pave a road away from misery was clearly outlined. We knew our goal. This was a definite step in the right direction.

Unwilling to calmly accept the possible failure of our bill, I researched other legislation that had a similar outcome. I came across a quote by Ronald Reagan that magnifies our plight: "We must reject the idea that every time a law's broken, society is guilty rather than the lawbreaker. It is time to restore the American precept that each individual is accountable for his actions."

Gathering more signatures, corresponding with more Assembly members, speaking with anyone who would listen to the details of Gavin's story, I was able to address numerous groups by just asking if I could talk about toughening hit-and-run penalties through Gavin's Law. Undoubtedly each time I finished speaking, tearful people from the crowd would approach me to regale stories of their relationships with Gavin. The television news did numerous interviews with our family. During this time, our entire family while knowing we were headed in the right direction seemed to be dangling on tether hooks.

As our mighty group returned to the Capitol building in January 2020, I was fearful the outcome would be unfavorable again. While waiting for the well-dressed, well-groomed Assembly members to take their respective seats, I kept flashing back on a favorite funny Gavin growing up story. Each year, a Christmas request from Gavin would be for an envelope filled with one-dollar bills. He didn't particularly care how much money was included if it was in one-dollar denominations only. When questioned about this odd request, he replied that he needed dollar bills to shop for clothing at the Salvation Army Store. Gavin had his own little quirks – the one-dollar bills were symbolic of clothing being simply a necessity, something to cover our bodies. That story kept running through my mind as we sat for this formal affair, all wearing our Gavin's Law T-shirts and jeans. What would Gavin think of all these machinations we were going through, while dressed in T-shirts and jeans? I could feel him smiling down on us from above.

On January 20, 2020, the Assembly Public Safety Committee passed AB 582 unanimously. The following week, Assembly Appropriations Committee also passed AB 582 unanimously. In mid-February, the Assembly floor voted 66 – 4 to pass our new bill. We were ready for the Senate next. Our journey was almost half over.

GAVIN'S LAW

Dedicated in Memory of Gavin Gladding

Gavin's Law – AB582

Gavin's Law passed the Public Safety Committee last Tuesday, January 14th! The next step is passing Appropriations scheduled for this Thursday, January 23rd. Rita and the Gladding Family thank you for your continued support of Gavin's Law!

For more information on AB 582, visit www.gavinslaw.com

When the early effects of an unknown virus, Covid 19, closed our state in mid-March 2020, all bills in progress, including Gavin's Law, came to a halt. We were told that only bills addressing the Covid issue would continue. Even so, through Gavin's magic and the work of Assemblyman Jim Patterson, our bill was able to ascend to the Senate Public Safety Committee. In August 2020, they heard AB 582, Gavin's Law, now renumbered AB 195, to meet Covid issues. During this time, the Capitol building was locked down and only principal witnesses could enter. Susan bravely went alone and gave her testimony again. Not being present in the committee room was very difficult for our family. We gathered at Gabrielle's home and watched the telecast of proceedings. Proponents phoned in to support Gavin's Law. Again, I could hear Gavin's voice and courage channeling through his nine-year-old daughter, Isla, when she called to ask the Senate Committee to please pass this law. "Gavin was my daddy." There were dozens of calls that the Senate committee allowed to be heard in support. Then the committee members began their remarks. When the last Senator on the committee, remarked, "This is an emotional issue but..." Our hearts began to sink. Then the vote was taken – three "yes" votes, one "no" vote, and three abstentions. We lost by one "no." We had advanced through two Assembly Committees and approval from the Assembly floor – 66 in favor, four not in favor – only to now lose by one vote in the first committee we faced in the Senate.

Our choices were to give up or wait until January 2021 to start all over again. I felt myself going into a state of shock. The passion I felt to defend our position in favor of Gavin's Law was not going to be calmed. I doubted I could ever again find peace. I couldn't rest. For the present, I knew I had to find a release. And thanks to both conviction and Gavin's touching manner, I did. The written word always tells a tale.

On Friday, August 14, 2020, The Fresno Bee printed an Editorial piece on the Opinion page entitled, "CA Senate opposes Gavin's Law named after dead Clovis man" The editorial was clearly in our favor, the esteemed editors clearly agreed that the defeat of Gavin's Law was appalling. An excerpt from the editorial read: "Californians remain at a greater risk of being hurt or killed by impaired drivers that leave the scene of their crime. And a young family in Clovis has to endure not only the loss of their husband and father but the bitterness of a political fight that should have been easy to win."

I sat down to write a response letter to the Editor of The Fresno Bee. To my gratification it was printed for their approximately 300,000 readers. On Sunday, September 6, 2020, my letter was published as the lead letter to the Editor that morning.

Gavin's Law is a No-Brainer

I support and praise the Fresno Bee Editorial Board for taking a positive stand regarding Assemblyman Jim Patterson's (R) AB 195, known as Gavin's Law. After being successful in moving AB 195 through two Assembly committees, and the Legislative floor, the Senate Public Safety Committee seemed to ignore the loophole that begs each Californian to open their eyes to wa. happening here. An innocent man was left to die. The hit-and-run driver spec. away knowing that by leaving the scene, sobering up, lawyering up five day. later, would carry a lessor penalty than felony DUI. Our current law encouraged unlicensed driver, Rogelio Alvarez Maravilla, to flee. Gavin wa. still alive. Rogelio left and was sentenced to 3 years. Free after only 12 months He could be driving down the street you are walking on right now.

This is a no brainer! Increase the penalty for fleeing the scene Arguments presented by the Senate Committee were insensitive including "the was an emotional issue". Of course, a man died! If that isn't enough to bring one's conscience to the table, then what could? Californians remain at risk. 10,000 Californians were in support of AB 195. Accountability Senators? Rita Gladding, Gavin Gladding's mother

The day after the Fresno Bee published my letter I received this email from a fellow bridge player, my friend: "Hello Rita, I am probably one of the last of an era that not only still gets the Bee but reads the letters to the editor. Your letter was so on point. I watched part of the hearing and was disheartened by their explanations for their votes. It wasn't going to change behavior, so why try? How about the victims and their families? I am so sorry for your loss and I know this kind of treatment by people that could actually help is so frustrating. Good for you giving his full name so people can remember what he [Rogelio] did. I wish you and Gary the best."

Shocked by the entire Sacramento experience, our family followed Susan's lead when she said to the news media, "This was just a bump in the road. We intend to keep moving forward." Our family believes that Gavin would want to attain justice for other Californians. Gavin *gone*. We continue to hope and pray for the passing of AB 582. No other family should have to suffer as we have or go through the intricate political process that followed. Gavin's Law is as far from a partisan issue as you can get. But, again, the political climate in the State of California depicts it as two disparate sides against each other, no matter the issue. In our case, the opposing side believes that extending prison sentences will not deter anyone from hitting and running, that when a driver flees the scene their decision is based on a fear that has nothing to do with their potential punishment. Our side does not claim that most hit-and-runners are aware of the laws or sentences, our argument is about achieving justice for the deceased's families. Restorative justice for the sake of those of us who believe the punishment should fit the crime. It's a shame that decency and humanity weren't enough to win our cause. Again, if we can ease the suffering of one more family, all will be worthwhile. We won't give up. Gavin will follow us. Always. His message in one of his appeal letters when he was River Park Camp Coordinator was "together we can turn our hopes into realities."

In 2021 I became the designated family spokesperson for Gavin's Law, now confusingly renumbered back to its original designation, AB 582. Life has that wonderful and/or eerie ability to continue advancing, but a dark cloud hung over me, following me around every corner. I knew a storm was coming, the only thing I didn't know was if the cloud would burst and let the sunshine through or if a cold rain would drench me amidst my hot tears. I prepared for both. I would welcome either. Another message from Abdoulraxman would soon be delivered. And, fortunately, it was.

We did start afresh. On April 6, 2021, we returned to face the Assembly Public Safety Committee once more. Assemblyman Jim Patterson presented AB 582 again, reapplying our terms to the bill and sticking to our original, simple stipulations – increase prison time from four to six years. "This is a balancing act between staying or leaving the scene of a crime," he explained. "The impulse to flee must be squelched." He seized the attention of the entire committee. Held in a separate room on the second floor of the building, I testified electronically wearing a mask covered with Texas Longhorns. We won even though there was one "no" vote submitted. Shocked by the win, I was escorted out of the Capitol building, my legs numb and a lump in my throat. I knew we had been granted the privilege to return. Key to success would be maintaining my strength. To keep holding our pattern of aggressively moving onward. I knew I could find that power again.

In mid-May 2021, we were to face on video the Assembly

Appropriations Committee for the second time. We had successfully made it through that committee with a unanimous vote in February 2020, but we were not as fortunate the next year. The committee did not put AB 582 to a vote. Instead, the bill went directly to the "Suspense File" where it can be held in perpetuity. The Appropriations Committee chair, Lorena Gonzalez, D, San Diego, ruled that our bill cannot be reintroduced until 2023, and to reappear the bill must be reconstructed, changed in a meaningful way. Unexpectedly, Ms. Gonzalez resigned on December 31, 2021. We are now pursuing the new chair to allow us to return in 2023. Another battle to fight but we intend to succeed. Our faith in justice is real. We WILL go on battling for Gavin's Law.

We will go back down a road that started out full of light but continues to grow dimmer. To live to witness your child's legacy unfold before you is something no parent should endure. I ask for the petitions of every Californian to reckon with advancing this penalty. Justice must serve others. We choose to continue to fight a system that has failed us. Statistics on hit-and-run deaths are not easy to track down, they are lumped in with pedestrian deaths. In California, in 2018, 3,798 pedestrians were killed. Gavin was one of them.

My final Letter to the Editor of the Fresno Bee, published July, 2021 read:

On Thursday, May 20, 2021, Assembly Bill 582, Gavin's Law, failed to move forward in Assembly Appropriations Committee. No explanation given. AB 582 had passed the entire Assembly in 2020 but fell one vote short in the Senate Public Safety Committee thus failing. Assemblyman Jim Patterson R – Fresno, authored AB 582 seeking to increase penalties for committing hit-and-run felonies from two – four years in prison, to four – six years. Gavin Gladding was a victim of hit-and-run driver, September 16, 2018. Abandoned on Friant

Road, Rogelio Alverez Maravilla sped away, hid for five days, sobered up, lawyered up as Crime Stoppers answered a tip to find the repaired truck attached to his father's home. Glass shards covered with my son's blood still inside.

Maravilla was incarcerated thirteen months. He's back driving your neighborhood. Reintroduced in April, 2021, AB 582 passed the Assembly Public Safety Committee. Assessment from Appropriations Committee cites raising prison time for hit-and-run accidents would increase incarceration costs "in the millions of dollars." Innocent Californians are at risk. The criminals find protection while the innocents become the victims. What will it take for our Assemblymen and Senators to understand the fact that this dangerous situation needs resolving?

Rita Gladding

March, 2019, our mighty group on steps of California Capital building,
Sacramento

CHAPTER SEVEN
THE GAVIN GLADDING FOUNDATION

"I consider his class to be the best I've taken to this day. His teaching was real,
applicable and practical...and most of all useful."
Caitlyn – Student at Clovis West High School
Excerpt from He Loved Us

Gavin's devoted friends joined us in a new goal: to create a 501(c)(3) corporation founded in Gavin's memory to carry on his legacy by protecting our environment and educating children. There was never any chance that Gavin would be forgotten. Too many people with tears in their eyes assured us of that fact. His death had enraged an entire community. Suddenly everyone seemed aware of the accident. I had a feeling that a movement with inexplicable energy was being born. There was a force at work. Emotions were running high and these feelings were not confined only to our family.

The community waited as five painfully agonizing days passed before Gavin's killer came forward. The news media updated his story four times a day. Knowing and realizing action needed to be taken, we began to take steps to form the Gavin Gladding Foundation, Inc. (GGF) in January 2019. It was Susan's mother, Aleane Butterworth (sorrowfully, now deceased) who first mentioned the need to do something permanently to honor Gavin. Feeling confident that the best attorney for the job would be a man named Chris, known in our valley for his skills in this particular area of creating non-profit corporations, he helped us get GGF rolling quickly. Chris believed that because our mission was to award monetary scholarships for students to forward their education, achieving non-profit status would be easier than usual. He was right. With his encouragement and expertise, along with the support of Susan, Gary, and Gavin's friends, Jerimiah, Brett and Urvi, we successfully received our non-profit status in record time. In June 2019 we became a recognized 501(c) (3) corporation, assigned as tax ID #84-2124387. The mission statement we adopted is short, clear, and concise. It is as follows:

The specific purpose of this corporation is to carry on the legacy of Gavin Gladding by inspiring youths to make the world a better place by providing scholarships and grants for higher education, camps and other educational programs focusing primarily on environmental stewardship.

Although attempting to pass Gavin's Law has been an extremely frustrating process, pulling the GGF together has been pure pleasure and a highly successful endeavor. Balancing the scales.

Shortly after its inception, GGF was approached by the organizers of our local Two Cities Marathon & Half that Gavin had participated in twice. Gavin had been training for his third marathon on the morning he was struck. Reaching out to us, the group that runs the race generously added "The Virtual Miracle Mile for Gavin Gladding" to the race, held in November 2018, just seven weeks after his death. #BeMoreLikeGavin, along with Gavin's photo, was printed on every entry bib. Runners were not charged an entry fee. This was the start of our association with The Two Cities Marathon & Half that has become an annual event. Four hundred people from our entire Central Valley participated in this part of the marathon honoring Gavin. Over $10,000 was raised to honor Gavin by his high school friend, Darren, who returned to his hometown from Los Angeles to run in place of Gavin.

Our entire family gathered to walk the last mile into Woodward Park together. There was also a virtual one mile walk for Gavin that had many of his Peace Corps buddies walking all around the world. The lead-off runners in Fresno were Carter and Isla. Both had sparkling eyes that morning. I found myself choking back tears until finally I was unable to stop crying during the entire mile. The kids from Fort Washington Elementary School turned out in droves. Families pushing baby strollers also took part in the event. We all proudly walked along together and crossed the finish line to honor Gavin's memory.

With unwavering determination, the GGF Board of Directors went on to develop a fundraising strategy to offer educational scholarships to students. Our foundation was a reality. Beginning with a golf tournament September 15, 2019, held at the golf course where Gavin was to join his buddies the day he was killed, 144 golfers came to play and pay tribute to him. High school friends returned to Fresno to play. His best friends since college returned to participate. Many of the teachers who he taught with joined in to pay tribute. The Eagle Springs Golf Course was alive with his spirit. Gavin's clubs were on the first hole allowing every participant to use his driver to start their game. Generous donations of food and drink kept our expenses low. Susan started the 144 golfers off with a speech that began with, "As you know, Gavin left to play golf Sunday, September 16. He didn't make the game. He never returned." Gavin *gone*. The event was remarkably heart-warming, and the funds raised exceeded our dreams.

Again, the community was behind us in honoring his legacy. To be an educator is a human endeavor requiring a special gift, both awesome and amazing. The GGF immediately set in motion another event for mid-May 2020, to honor the first birthday that Gavin wouldn't be sharing with those he left behind.

And then there was COVID 19. It seemed our Earth stopped turning on its axis. All events cancelled. The State of California shut down on March 13, 2020. Fundraising came to a halt.

With great euphoria, GGF was still able to fund two 2020 Clovis West seniors after graduation ceremonies were cancelled. Plans for a second golf tournament were scrapped for September 2020. With conviction, courage and strength the tournament was rescheduled to the Fall 2021. Our website, www.gavingladdingfoundation.org, is up and running. Communication with Gavin's followers is still available. As of this writing, the Board is searching for other ways to raise money. I have no doubt that we will continue toward our goal of granting academic scholarships into eternity. Gavin would have wanted this gift to endure. Undoubtedly, this was part of the message Abdoulraxman was ordained to convey.

California 501(C)(3) Corporation
Tax I.D. #84-2185387

Two Cities Marathon bib for Gavin Gladding Memorial Mile, 2018. Now a perpetual event

Photo taken at Inaugural GGF Golf Tournament, 2019. Note shaft of light that appears where Gavin would be standing

CHAPTER EIGHT
GAMBIARISING

"Mr. Gladding was a kind and supportive teacher. He possessed a wealth of knowledge and would share wonderful stories about his time in The Gambia."
Gardenia – Student at Clovis West High School
Excerpt from He Loved Us

While still in the midst of a pandemic in August 2020, we were approached by one of Gavin's best friends from his Gambian Peace Corps tour, Dr. Kevin Moore. He is yet another friend of Gavin's who shares the passion for improving the world through education and kindness. Kevin is currently on staff at UC San Diego Health, Department of Radiation. He has a Ph.D., is a Diplomat of the American Board of Radiology, board certified in Therapeutic Medical Physics, and now Professor of Medical Physics in the department of Radiation and Medicine at University of California, San Diego.

This is an excerpt from Kevin's Facebook post the day after Gavin was killed, September 19, 2018: "I have no idea how to start this. How do you begin a post that has to simultaneously introduce and then eulogize one of the best people you've ever known? Gavin Gladding was one of those big-hearted people that creates their own social gravitational field into which everyone will be inexorably pulled. One day (probably the day after you met him) you will wake up and realize you love Gavin Gladding. He was warm, kind, understanding, curious, wickedly funny and as good a person one could hope to encounter in this world."

Gambiarising was founded by the previous Peace Corps Director of The Gambia, Mike McConnell. Since 2011 they have worked to raise funds to pay for thousands of Gambian students' school fees and to provide supplemental food assistance. These two obstacles continue to be perpetual problems that limit the horizons of Gambian children, especially girls. Our agreement is to partner with the Gambiarising project and by joining hands in this collaboration, GGF will achieve international reach as part of our mission to educate youth. For many years, the village of Sare Samba has been a Peace Corps training village. They speak Wolof, the same dialect as Gavin's village, Charmen. Kevin is positive that he and Gavin visited this training village together.

Kevin has offered our GGF Board the opportunity to contribute on multi-levels of support in honor of Gavin. The GGF has agreed to donate a substantial monetary gift for the next five years. A link from our website, gavingladdingfoundation.org is in the works. Donations can be made directly to us and will be presented in Gavin's name. There will be more information on their website, www.gambiarising.org. New opportunities continue to emerge, ensuring that Gavin won't be forgotten, that his life was not in vain. His magic will always be carried on. Now on two different continents.

GGF joined with another non-profit, GambiaRising, supporting students in The Gambia, West Africa, with school supplies and food

CHAPTER NINE
IN GAVIN'S WORDS

"You don't realize how special something is until you no longer have it. Not having Mr. Gladding around will be tough but he had a positive impact on everybody." Nick – Student at Clovis West High School
Excerpt from He Loved Us

Gavin was always composing poems and sending letters. I try not to handle these fragile, hand printed letters much these days. Gavin, like myself, was left-handed and his script was just about unreadable, but I cherish each tiny scrap of his handwriting. Another letter from him will never arrive. Gavin, *gone.*

Valentine's Day of his senior year in high school, I received a little poem from him. I breathe these words of his in deeply every day. Gavin might have written this, but little did he know that I would have chosen the same words to say to him:

When I leave and go away,

You and I both know,

I won't be going there to stay,

I will never let you go.

Gavin's funny approach to serious matters always brought us joy and made us smile. As a freshman at UCSB he wrote to the entire family: "I greatly appreciate how lucky I have been having you. Even though sometimes I don't show my appreciation and love for all of you it is always there. Love, the Recipient of Checks."

We received only a few letters from Gavin while serving in the Peace Corps. After he was there for a short while, the telephone became an easier option. But it was always a treat to find a letter in our mailbox and I saved each one in the original "package" used to mail it. Many also had rolls of film included so the packaging was a Gavin design. A brown paper cut up grocery bag would serve as the base for the innovative envelope. Gavin had many times communicated with us that the most important thing to have in The Gambia was duct tape. His envelopes always were sealed with it, and all worked. One film roll container arrived with sand from his trip to the Sahara Dessert. It is on proud display in his old room today. Gavin was always original with whatever he did.

I love his description of the first time he taught a class of 9th grade children. Seems like providence now that, in his few correspondences, he would include this account from August 29, 1998: "Two days ago, I had to teach at the Kwinella Jr. Secondary School. It was the first time I had to teach so I was kind of distraught about what I would teach and how it would go. I taught 9th grade, the highest grade, so I picked a topic that I was interested in and knew about. I taught them about the tides, which is a very difficult concept to grasp. I thought it was appropriate because the Gambia River is tidally influenced all the way up. After over an hour of lecturing and group activity they understood it, so I took the entire experience as a victory. Not bad considering I had to teach: Gravity, the Earth/Sun/Moon relationship, and the properties of water to 9th grade African school kids."

In a letter to his sister dated September 25, 1998, Gavin sent the following message regarding our family's upcoming Thanksgiving dinner: "Gab, I have a request. You know how we say what we are thankful for: well DON'T TELL MOM OR DAD OR ANYBODY: read this when it's my turn: Any length of space or time can never keep you from those you love-long as you keep them close to your heart. Through this I am with you there tonight and you are with me. What am I thankful for this Thanksgiving, 1998? I am thankfully realizing that the world is a really big place and there is nowhere I would rather be than sitting there at that table. I am thankful for the commencement of my extended stay at the University of California Santa Barbara. I am thankful that the people gathered here loved me enough to let me go off and pursue my dreams. I am thankful that the Sisters Di Bella married off one of their own. I am thankful for everyone's health and happiness. I am thankful that right now I am having dinner at the Ambassador's house with all the other Americans in The Gambia. A quote from The Count of Monte Christo, regarding a conversation I just had with a mother who just saw her son go into military service in Africa, 'He will increase in strength and honor by struggling with adversity, which he will convert into prosperity. Leave him to build up the future for you and I venture to say you will confide it to safe hands.' The things in life are many, the ones that matter are few. I love you all, Gavin."

Gavin described in detail, using drawings he made, the most efficient mode of transportation, the bush taxi: "But on the North bank all of the bush taxis I have seen are pickup trucks that look like this: On top you put luggage, bikes, 50 lb. bags of salt, drums, vases, goats (no really, I've seen goats strapped to the roofs of these things. You just hope they aren't peeing on your bag), trees, etc. Pretty much anything of size because inside they can legally have 14 people. This is comparable to squeezing 4 people along the backseat of Dad's Buick. Oh yeah the lady next to you has a 5 lb. sack of fish and on the other side is a woman breast feeding."

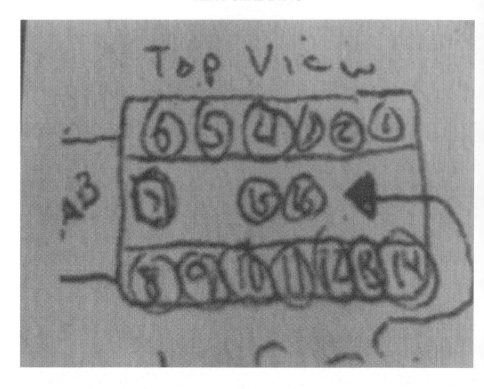

Also included in that letter is an account of the first funeral Gavin attended. Again, since we have so few written words from him to this day I find it curious why he would include this account: "I went to my first Gambian funeral yesterday. The men go and dig the hole (and I accompanied them throughout all of this) in the cemetery. The body is not laid on its' back. It is laid on its' right side so the hole is small and skinny. They bury people here on their right side. Why?? I don't know. After the hole is dug they cut trees to make boards to lay across the top. After the grave is prepared the men go and get the body with a horse cart, take it to the mosque, say a short prayer, then proceed to the grave, bury the body, say a prayer, return as a group to the mosque and pray once more. I did not see the women all day. In this culture it is a sign of weakness, and almost a bad omen to cry. NO ONE CRIES."

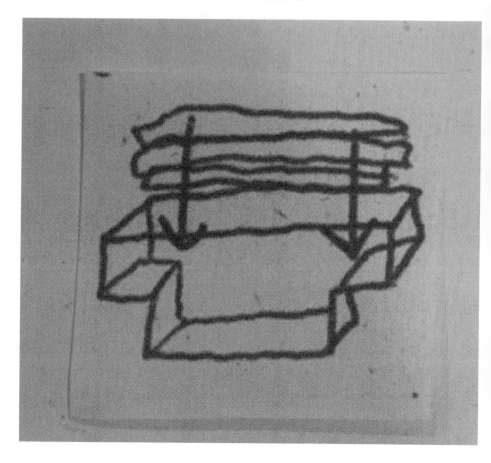

It is baffling to fathom how different cultures grieve and show emotion. As mothers, the thing we each share is the unbearable fear of losing a child. To hold back tears at this time is unimaginable to me. How is a grieving parent capable of that kind of control? From the instant I picked up the phone to hear Gabrielle say, "There's been an accident. It's Gavin," my tears began to flow. Hot and heavy. Somehow or other, I grabbed hold of my Rosary dismissing the thought that tears were even necessary. This had to be a minor accident. Why should I be crying? Tears are deemed to cleanse the soul. There was no need for that now. God would protect Gavin and never take him from us so soon. I could not accept a different aftereffect. When Gary began to push harder on the gas pedal, he also didn't cry. Instead, he chanted "take me, not him" during the entire trip back to Fresno. I actually looked at him and said "God isn't taking anyone. Especially Gavin." His chant was incomprehensible to me.

Alexander Dumas' Count of Monte Christo is one of my favorite books. I sent it off to Gavin hoping he would learn from it, as I had. In a letter arriving in late fall of Gavin's first year in the Peace Corps, he included this postscript: "1/2 way through the Count of Monte Christo. It's revenge time for Dantes!" Gavin had the finite perception to understand the heart of the novel. The story of injustice it contained always touched me. An honest man whose life becomes shattered by the deception of another man and his family. Was I drawn to this classic due to some sort of foreboding of unspeakable things to come? Today I like to think no, of course not. In the end, Edmond Dante's does find justice. Nevertheless, the story now haunts me more than ever. I am honored to know Gavin liked it enough to use this quote from the story in a conversation he had with a Gambian mother bidding farewell to her son as he entered military service: "He will increase in strength and honor by struggling with adversity, which he will convert into prosperity. Leave him to build up the future for you, and I venture to say you will confide it to safe hands." Justice will triumph.

We received this quote in an email from Gavin sent on September 24 2016, two years to the day before his funeral service: *"Focus on the journey, no the destination. Joy is found not in finishing an activity but in doing it." Greg Anderson*

Perhaps my favorite letter from Gavin arrived on a plain white sheet o paper dated December 8, 1998: "Dear Rita and Gary Gladding, Thank you for being such wonderful people/parents. Merry Christmas, Gavin Gladding"

CHAPTER TEN
NEVER SAYING GOODBYE

"With a big smile across his face, Mr. Gladding would brighten your day. He led by example. Devoted, caring and welcoming."
Andriana – Student at Clovis West High School
Excerpts from He Loved Us

An unexpected early morning phone call can suddenly snap one back to the absoluteness of the real world. The caller was Danny, Gavin's best friend during his years at the University of California, Santa Barbara. It had been almost two years since Gavin's funeral service before I heard from Danny again. One great gift of having 2,000 people attend Gavin's funeral was being able to look into the tear-filled eyes of his best college buddy, whom we hadn't seen since they graduated in 1998. Words escaped both of us. Tears and hugs were all that was needed. The morning Danny called two years later was no different – cell phone to cell phone, we both still had no words. Only long gasps for air between our sobs. Of the hundreds of cards, we gratefully received after Gavin was killed, the only one I still keep on my desk is Danny's. His heartfelt words touched me. In the first bleak months, I reread it often: "Gavin was my best friend in life. There are no words to express how sorry I am for your loss. We all loved Gavin so much and he impacted our lives so much. It's impossible to replace that void. He will be missed but never forgotten."

Gavin and Danny at Gavin's Wedding 9/5/04

That surprising and unexpected phone call from Danny awakened within me the need to write the story of my amazing son and his impact on others. I have lacked the courage to put anything on paper until now. Reliving these events is terrible for a mother who has lost a child. I ache as if it were yesterday. To experience the woe of losing a child is... well, to quote Annette, my good friend of almost fifty years who witnessed her daughter lose the battle to survive a very aggressive cancerous brain tumor, "There are no words." She has said this to me over and over. Since that day, it's become our special way of communicating about the loss of our children. Only a mother who has lost a child knows how deeply that resonates with another in the same club. And it is a club we all belong to together. The unwritten rules contain knowing that there is strength to be gleaned from others who have had their hearts torn.

As the days since our loss have turned into weeks, then months, and now years, the pure disbelief that accompanies knowing the death of a child is not the natural order of things will always remain. Parents first, not their children. This is just a concept that starts as impossible to grasp, to become even harder to believe. And, most importantly, in the beginning it lies outside the realm of reality. However, what does remain becomes the necessity to accept and remember. And forgive. Finding that every day becomes a tiny bit easier to acknowledge what has happened, sheds light from without as well as within.

To return to the memories I share now is both bitter and sweet. From within this story is the inspiration I found in the powerful force that was Gavin. Can a mother ever really know her son? I could always feel that he possessed a certain magnetism of drawing people to him. Now the world would never get to fully experience this sparkle. God reached out his hand and my son truly became Gavin 'Gone' Gladding.

I fear that I will not be able to remember his face during all the 43 years leading up to this senseless death at the hands of a hit-and-run driver.

Deep in some dark corner of my closet is a bag that holds the clothes I was wearing when I last saw Gavin. These include a black cap boasting a pink breast cancer survivor ribbon and pink flip-flops. They remain unwashed, untouched since September 16, 2018. Knowing they are there provides me with the resolution to advance in the correct direction. These articles have become an everlasting testimony to the reality of September 16, 2018.

One of the most heart-wrenching sights of that initial week without Gavin was watching Oscar, the family Labradoodle, laying before the front door. He lifted his head in anticipation each time the door opened. Slowly, he would return his head to the floor. I knew who he was looking for. Their ashes are mixed together forever providing each with the comfort of the other. As it should be.

We've continued to understand Gavin's reach and legacy. Two years after his death, my grandson, Jett, a Junior at Buchanan High School, received this correspondence from his Advanced Placement Environmental Studies teacher, dated August 21, 2020: "Hello! I did my student teaching at Clovis West when Gavin was there. I was fortunate to observe his classroom a few times when he was teaching APES. He made me want to teach this course. The excitement that he has about the subject matter was something I always admired, and I hope to replicate. He had so much influence on a ton of people in and around the district I am proud to say that he influenced the way I teach."

Close to three years since Gavin's death, my granddaughter Finley entered her first class of high school as a freshman. Her teacher, the same sweet man that had sent us the above text, approached her, asking if Gavin was her uncle. His face quivered as if close to tears. She stood tall and straight, looked into his tear-filled eyes and answered, "Yes."

In 2020, I made a Christmas shopping trip to secure a present for a special friend. Choosing Holiday Boutique, an exquisite gift store operated by a guild of Valley Children's Hospital – all proceeds go to the hospital – a beautiful woman was ready to charge me for my purchase. Checking to see if I was in their system, I gave her my name. The woman behind the counter froze, her eyes filling with tears. I immediately could sense her heartfelt emotions. I looked at her, choked, and said one word, "Gavin." With tears running down both of our faces, she explained that she had worked with him at Fort Washington Elementary School. She said, "I have never worked with a better man." Her remembrance of my son reassures me that his powerful magic will endure forever. Tears give way to smiles. Smiles that fill my heart with warmth.

I write this account as a demonstration of the strength, hope, trust, and courage needed to forge ahead to make both Gavin's life and death meaningful. It won't change what happened, but it can change what we hope to be Gavin's legacy. It is a testimony to how we allowed and trusted the belief both to accept, then work alongside and ultimately conquer our heartache the whole way. Gavin truly co-existed through a shining light.

Gavin's house in The Gambia

Photo taken by Gavin on the River Niger, Mali, Africa on route to Timbuktu.

Timbuktu Temple

CHAPTER ELEVEN
EPILOGUE

"He had the power to spark curiosity in his students.
He was the reason I choose to pursue a career in science."
Michael – Student at Clovis West High School
Excerpt from, 'He Loved Us"

I awaken each morning, roll over, and immediately remember, *oh yes, he's still gone.* I have known from the day he left us there was the prospect that every day I would be living the first day of his death all over again. What I was unsure about was that I possessed the ability to continue advancing– always forward – which would have to come from within.

Living this repetitive narrative has opened my eyes to a world I feel compelled to impact. Gavin's story needs to be shared. His demise must open eyes to the need of accountability for one's actions in the state of California. Endless accounts of hit-and-run incidents pepper the pages of California newspapers. To ignore this truth is to ignore the lives of the thousands of innocent individuals who are struck and left behind each year.

By making Gavin's goals an active part of our lives, I find, within the workings of his Foundation and trying to pass this law, I continue on an avenue of forgiveness. I own up to the brutality he suffered at the hands of misdirected, scared individuals. The realization that three individuals walk the planet and Gavin is deceased at their hands will always haunt me. This is a hard pill to swallow. I have learned that through forgiveness I gain the strength to continue with his mission and to continue to find the inner peace to allow me to finish my years on Earth. With continued strength, hard work and backing, Gavin's goals continue to become a reality.

In 2018, 3,798 pedestrians were killed in California. In 2020, there was a 4.8% increase over 2019 pedestrian deaths, totaling 6,612. Today, hit-and-run accidents continue to increase in our state. If a lesson is learned through this entire muddy process, it is that Gavin's death can and will serve to assist other families of hit-and-run victims. Gavin is a spirit that continues to motivate so many people on many levels. His death also led to the formation of the Gavin Gladding Foundation, Inc. to ensure that his inheritance, the sharing of knowledge, will serve as a source of empowerment to others for years to come.

Our struggle to pass Gavin's Law will prove good can triumph over iniquity. We will also continue our uphill campaign to find the success needed to make Gavin's Law a reality. Hit-and-run penalties must be increased in the state of California. His achievements will live forever in the hearts of an entire community that expected him to help resolve problems. A phrase he used frequently was, "We'll figure it out." I believe he is right.

Along with Gavin's inspirational words, his soul rests within me for all eternity.

Messenger from God, Abdoulraxman, we love you, and will always suffer the loss of your being. We will wonder for all eternity what your message was meant to be. Peace? Kindness? Justice? Or was it something much deeper? God knows, but the rest of us can just venture guesses.

Knowing my son, reading the letters written by his students after his death, I'm drawn back to the many words said about him: passionate, happy, confident, kind, impactful, inspirational. This is his legacy. This is why he will never be forgotten. We were extraordinarily lucky to have been able to witness his magic as an educator and inspiring human being for 43 years, 4 months and 3 days. I love you my Gavin "Gone" Gladding.

I leave you with these wise words by my friend Linda Glassman, from the book Words Worth Sharing:

Look forward, not backwards.
Do not fear the unknown.
Seek the help of those you love.
Believe in yourself.
Never lose sight of your goal.

CHAPTER TWELVE
TESTIMONY

"He led by example devoted, caring, and welcoming to all. An inspirational mentor and Clovis West favorite, Mr. Gladding will forever remain in our hearts."

Andriana - Student at Clovis West High School

Excerpt from He Loved Us

As the final chapter in this book, I feel the need to share with my readers a sampling of many of the wonderful sentiments written about Gavin since he passed. I accept as true these many heart felt, sometimes gut-wrenching testimonials that stand to corroborate my very own personal perspectives on Gavin's unique gifts to this world.

97 letters were written when Gavin's Clovis West High School students learned of his death. Another 300 plus were written by the elementary students at Fort Washington Elementary School. A collection called *He Loved Us – Stories of Mr. Gladding by the Students Who Loved Him* - was lovingly collected and compiled by Rhonda Parr Schafer during the immediate days following Gavin's death. The writings of these students assure me that Gavin will always be remembered. I've also included several articles from the Fresno Bee, which did a wonderful job of telling our story to the public.

But first, I offer you Gavin's favorite recipe from the Gambia as a token of my appreciation for your attention. Submitted by Mike Imodio, one of Gavin's fellow Gambian Peace Corp Volunteers, this special recipe is written as if everyone could figure it out! Reminds me of Italian recipes passed down from my mother and aunts. Mike presently lives in Milan, Italy. He flew in to attend Gavin's funeral service.

THE GAMBIAN BLACK-EYED PEA SANDWICH

1 bag black eyed peas
2 onions, chopped
Peanut, vegetable or palm oil from The Gambia
1 can tomato paste
2 beef bouillon cubes

Soak black eyed peas overnight Boil for 1 hour. Drain.
Sauté onions in oil. Add bouillon cubes. Cook down leaving a little water in pot. Put beans back in. Stir then mash (should be somewhat liquefied).
Add onions.
Add Salt & Pepper.
Add more oil if mixture appears dry.
Mash with 1 can tomato paste. Stir well. Using good bread, make sandwiches!

REMEMBERING MR. GLADDING:
Testimonies from students at Clovis West High School and Ft. Washington Elementary School

Sophia – I had Mr. Gladding for AP Environmental Science my junior year in 2016. His class was literally one of the first things that made me want to pursue a career in justice. I know he deliberately did a section on environmental justice to show students that the victories of today cannot cloud the work tomorrow. I know I am not the only student whose life had been forever altered by his teaching. I pray for your family's healing and eventual peace in the wake of this. He was a good man and a good friend to Mother Earth. He raised a generation to love each other and love the Earth. He raised us to stop and look outside our window and see how much beauty and divinity is in the way the sun shines alone. Not even death can take that away from him.

Nathan – Truly inspirational human being. First bonded over our mutual love for camping and for the song "Better Together" by Jack Johnson. He was passionate about everything he did, and he showed it through his teachings. We once took a hike together with a few students up at Millerton Lake. I was in awe of how much beauty he knew about God's creation. He wrote a recommendation letter for my college application without any hesitation. He was a great man, teacher, and role model. Love always, Nathan Blitz.

Sarah – The essence of who Mr. Gladding was, is hard to accurately capture in words. He was an educator, a father, an inspiration, and yet still so much more. When students walked into his classroom, and stress or anger from the day melted away. Reflecting upon the APES class which he taught, I cannot pinpoint a certain great memory, but instead remember a feeling of overwhelming joy, wonderment, and luck, to have been introduced to this incredible individual. Recently, I took up an interest in applying to the Peace Corps, and decided to email Mr. Gladding for some advice. Even though he had not been my teacher for four years, and probably had not seen him for two years, Mr. Gladding's response was to give me his personal number and tell me to call him whenever with questions. That was simply the kind of person he was: someone who went above and beyond every chance he got. Gavin Gladding will be deeply missed.

Delaney – I first met Mr. Gladding while I was attending River Camp over the summer in elementary school. He was one of the lead counselors and I always remembered how friendly he was and how he would make sure that everyone was included and having a great time. All of us at camp loved him and he brought such a great energy with him every single day. Years went by and I ended up attending Clovis West. When I decided to take AP Environmental Studies my junior year, I was so surprised and excited to see that Mr. Gladding was the teacher. From then on, he was without a doubt the most influential teacher I had while attending Clovis West. In June I earned my degree in Environmental Management at Cal Poly SLO as a result of his guidance and passion for the subject, he even wrote me a letter of recommendation when I was applying to schools. He cared deeply for his students and was willing to offer help wherever it was needed, whether school related or personal. He helped me decide what I wanted to do with my life at a time when I felt lost and overwhelmed by college applications. Mr. Gladding had a tremendous impact on my life, and the smile and enthusiasm that he greeted us with every day of class will never be forgotten. I will now strive to share the passion for the environment that he shared with me in his memory.

Ashley – Mr. Gladding ignited a passion for justice within me that I never realized I could have. He encouraged us to form our own opinions, based off facts of course. His passion for life easily fell on all his students and his impact on the world around him created so many ripples in my life and the lives of others who took his classes, knew him as a person. His heart for justice itself changed my life. I had higher expectations of people and the world around me. I stuck up for others who couldn't because Mr. Gladding taught me that I could do so and be successful. I decided to get a degree in nonprofit management largely because of my passion for justice that Mr. Gladding ignites. This degree didn't just impact my career, but the people I know, the perspective I now have, and the advocacy work I now strive to involve others in. I'm so grateful for the impact he made in so many lives. And I know I'll always remember him as the person who changed mine.

Jon – He was the best teacher I ever had! Always pushed me to be a better student, which at the time I didn't realize why he would do it, but I soon realized if it wasn't for him I would've not been ready for Santa Clara. My favorite memory was not even a memory, it was just how supportive he was with me and any other student he taught. He always greeted you with a smile, whether he was having a bad day or a good one. You could never tell. He made a very challenging class exciting to come to everyday, and his personality, and how great of a guy he was is what I'm going to miss most. He had a positive impact on more students than any other teacher at Clovis West. I am in my senior year at Santa Clara and will graduate in June with a degree in Environmental Science. I currently work for the Oakland A's on the grounds crew that focuses on the sustainability of the Oakland Coliseum. Mr. Gladding wrote my letter of recommendation to Santa Clara and I am truly grateful.

Kevin – Hi, I would like to share a message about Mr. Gladding.

Thank you for being the best teacher I ever had. You made learning fun and had a positive attitude every single day. I loved how you didn't go by the book to accomplish what you needed. I will always admire that.

Emma – I remember Mr. Gladding as one of the most kind, passionate, and inspiring people I have met. He always knew what to say or do: be it through knowing how to offer advice or wisdom. One of my favorite memories is when a group of friends and I were goofing around after a test in his class and trying to read each other's tarot cards for relationship advice. Mr. Gladding, witty and personable as always, came up to us to get his own cards read. After joking around with us he gave us some real-life advice, talking about his love for his family and wife, and how we could attain something as amazing as he had. That was Mr. Gladding: always taking the time to connect with his students and making sure he had a positive impact in their lives. I can confidently speak for everyone when I say that is exactly what he did; everyone that met Mr. Gladding is better off for it. I am so thankful to have known Mr. Gladding and I will always remember the goodness that radiated from him. It is a joy that his students will go on carrying and a joy that will vibrantly live on in his memory.

Alexa – I was never lucky enough to have him as a teacher and I had him as a friend during school. It was a particularly hard day during my freshman year at Clovis West and he saw me crying in the parking lot when I found out my brother who was overseas was involved in a bombing, he told me to come sit in his classroom and talk for as long as I needed. He had no idea who I was, just saw I was in need and wanted to be there for a student. I think that speaks volumes about the kind of person he was. I never forgot about that day, and I will never forget about him.

Brittney – I remember leaving a conversation I had with Mr. Gladding confident, happy and blissful. The thing is every conversation I've ever had with Mr. Gladding ended this way. He just had a talent of making people happier with his kindness, smile and laughter.

Jenae – He has the power to spark curiosity in his students. Gavin changed my life, shaped me as a person. I will be forever grateful to him and his family. He will be remembered always.

Kennedy – There wasn't a day I didn't look forward to his class and experience his teaching. He is inspirational, kind-hearted, and passionate.

Devon (Ft. Washington father) – He asked the children to never underestimate the power of the word "YET." He asked the children to start using the word "YET" after every sentence beginning in "I can't." For example, "I can't read at that level YET." Such awesome advice.

Aaron – He was a great teacher as well as an incredible guy. He is one of the teacher's that helped me grow out of my antisocial shell.

Beth – I will always remember Mr. Gladding as the kind, positive, funny, nature- loving guy I got to know during our Costa Rica trip. {Gavin applied for and received a grant to take eight students to Costa Rica} I hold my memories of Mr. Gladding from that trip close to my heart. He impacted me and so many others beyond the classroom, showing us what it looks like to have passion for what we do and be kind to others. He is so missed.

Robert Romanacce – Attending the dedication of Fort Washington's 2018-19 yearbook was the Chief Deputy District Attorney that had been through all the Fresno County Court appearances representing our family. Although he usually only represents homicide cases, he wanted to take on

Gavin's defense. His son went to Fort Washington and greeted Robert and Roman each morning. His text to Susan, Gabrielle and I on yearbook reveal day read: "Ladies… thank you for allowing me the honor of serving your family and the memory of Gavin. I hope the minimal amount of atonement we achieved through the court process will bring you all a bit of solace over your loss. In 23 years as an attorney, I've never seen such an outpouring of love and affection over the loss of a man's life. And yet it appears he still lives on in the minds and hearts of those that he touched. Truly remarkable. Be well."

FORT WASHINGTON ELEMENTARY SCHOOL YEARBOOK 2018 – 2019 - "It is with honor we dedicate the 2018-19 Fort Washington Yearbook to Mr. Gavin Gladding. Mr. Gavin Gladding was one of the most genuine individuals that one could meet. He always carried a warm smile on his face.

Mr. Gladding was always kind-hearted and showed much empathy. Therefore, he always found meaningful ways to guide students to change their behavior and to learn from the experiences.

Mr. Gladding was the type of individual that always looked for the good in any individual. Mr. Gladding was a person of integrity and believed in clarity. We are blessed to have had the past two years to work alongside Mr. Gladding and learn the positive impact one could have in any community."

Brianna – (5th Grade Student at Fort Washington Elementary school and her family) – "Whenever someone was in trouble, Mr. Gladding would always be nice and talk to them about what they did and how to make it better without making them feel like they were in trouble. He was always so kind and told jokes at morning announcements. He made our school a better place. He always gave everybody high-fives. He was my favorite person that worked at the school. Our memories of him are un-erasable like a sharpie on our hearts."

Finn – (co-worker with Gavin at RiverCamp) "He was someone who I wished I could ask so many questions and spent more time with him. I wish I got to know him more. Our memories were always good, including canoeing with his two kids down the river for a River Camp training in 2015, also included lots of water play and rope swinging. He was truly the best of the best, a perfect human being. He touched so many lives, and I will work hard to be a better human in his memory." With a heavy heart and much love, Finn

EXCERPTS FROM THE FRESNO BEE'S CONTINUOUS COVERAGE

Sunday, February 9, 2020:

Fresno Widow Fights For Tougher Hit-And-Run Sentences

Susan Gladding was never one to take on causes. Never one to make public speeches. Or serve as a source of strength and inspiration to others. Those traits belonged to her husband, Gavin, a well-liked Clovis Unified administrator and former Peace Corps volunteer. Susan despite his frequent encouragement, preferred to stay in the background. Where she always felt more comfortable.

"Gavin was a natural in front of people," Susan Gladding said. "That is where he thrived." That all changed following the tragic events of Sept. 16, 2018, when Gavin was struck from behind by a pickup truck while running on the shoulder of Friant Road shortly before 6 a.m. The driver fled the scene, and Gladding died from his injuries after being rushed to Community Regional Medical Center. Before turning himself into the police five days later, 18-year-old Rogelio Alvarez Maravilla replaced a broken windshield and side mirror and deleted potentially incriminating text messages, according to court documents. The unlicensed Alvarez Maravilla received a three-year jail sentence - one shy of the maximum penalty for hit-and-run fatalities under California law - but only served 12 months. He is already a free man.

Legal Loophole

Compounding the loss of her partner and their two children, Susan Gladding couldn't wrap her head around the light sentence. Especially when she found out a legal loophole that practically incentivizes drunken drivers to flee the scene of an accident in order to avoid facing harsher DUI penalties. But how can one voice, or even one family's voice, effect change?

It's funny but I remember looking at the Sierras and thinking, "What do you do about this? It's like moving a mountain," Susan Gladding recalled. "That's how the system is. Even though I've got all this frustration, what am I going to do?" It would have been easy for Susan to curl up into a ball and shut out the world. Instead, with support from Gavin's family, her tight circle of friends and Fresno Assemblyman Jim Patterson, Susan is honoring her late husband's memory and fighting for victims like her.

Gavin's law, which would increase penalties for hit-and-run drivers who flee an accident that results in injury or death, passed the Assembly floor 66 - 3 vote on January 27 and will soon be taken up by the Senate.

The future of 582 is less than assured because it goes against the grain. In recent years Sacramento law makers have worked to reduce the state's overcrowded prisons by decreasing criminal sentences.

Powerful Voice

But the bill would never have made it this far without Susan Gladding's powerful testimony before the Assembly Public Safety Committee in March 2019. Gladding's words brought many in the room to tears, swaying the votes of several members of Democratic-controlled committee not normally inclined to support legislation that enhances criminal penalties or advances a Republican sponsored bill. During the hearing Chairman Reginald Jones-Sawyer, D-Los Angeles, credited Gladding with "basically turning" the committee and called her "the most powerful speaker for your cause...that we ever had.

"I've been in a lot of committee meetings and presented a lot of material, and I've never seen anything like this before," said Patterson, who authored the bill but has since taken on two Democratic colleagues as co sponsors. "What we found out was that Susan could easily read hearts and minds and actually change votes."

Susan Gladding, along with Gavin's parents, Gary and Rita, and sister Gabrielle Ruby have made four trips to Sacramento to attend Assembly hearings and witness votes. The process starts all over again since Gavin's Law has advanced to the Senate. It's been a lot for anyone to handle, even though Gavin always knew his wife was capable of leading causes, giving public speeches and inspiring others. Now Susan Gladding knows it, too.

"I feel like he's looking down on me saying, 'Told you so,' she said. "I feel like he's giving me strength I didn't have before."

Sunday, September 28, 2020

Gavin Gladding's Widow On Law Meant To Honor Her Husband

Editor's note: Gavin Gladding, a Clovis Unified Administrator, was jogging in the early morning in northeast Fresno on Sept. 16, 2018, when he was killed by a drunken driver who left the scene. In this Valley Voice essay, Gavin Gladding's widow, Susan Gladding, relates the experience to get a law passed in her husband's honor...

It has been two years since we lost Gavin. In that time, we have leaned on each other to get through birthdays, holidays and family celebrations - occasions that will never be the same without our husband, father, son, brother and friend.

Thanks to a great deal of faith, hope and a community that has surrounded us with love, we persevered. We found ways to keep Gavin's memory alive - to champion causes we know he would support. We started the Gavin Gladding Foundation to help local students pay for college and support other experimental educational opportunities. We also embarked upon the greatest, most exciting and intensely frustrating foray into the legislative process - Gavin's Law. When we realized there was a loophole in state law that actually benefits drunken drivers who leave the scene of an accident, we knew we had to do something to close it. Shockingly, drivers that leave the scene and sober up before their arrest can avoid the 15-year maximum sentence of a felony DUI conviction. A four-year sentence is the most they will face.

Following the accident that took Gavin's life, the groundswell of support was overwhelming. More than 10,000 people signed our petition for Gavin's Law. Voices from here at home and across the state gave us all the confidence in the world that this common-sense legislation would sail through unopposed. After all, who can be against fixing such a glaring failure in the law?

What we didn't know — what most people don't know — is that common-sense reforms like the ones proposed in Gavin's Law often don't often make it past the first committee hearing because of partisan politics. We defied the odds on our legislative journey, starting with the first hearing in the Assembly Public Safety Committee in 2019. The partisan conclusion was reached before the hearing — Gavin's Law would die on a party-line vote without any Democratic support.

Sitting in the audience at the Capitol that day, I was well prepared to go home defeated. After we explained the dangerous loophole, we all watched with amazement as a couple of Democrat members of the committee agreed with us. After listening to the facts we presented about the loophole, Assemblyman Bill Quirk ignored the directive to vote against the bill. Another member even went a step further and asked to amend the bill slightly so she could vote for it. Eventually it passed unanimously out of the committee.

This kind of think outside-the-box mentality is lost on the people making laws in California, especially when it comes to victims' rights. Democrat Assembly members turned partisan rhetoric to support our common-sense changes — ones we hope they will support once again when Gavin's Law is reintroduced by Assemblyman Jim Patterson next year.

In the end, Gavin's Law failed to make it out of the Senate Public Safety Committee, failing one vote short. To say we were disappointed would be an understatement. It seemed like we were finally breaking past the partisan barrier that lays waste to so many good reforms. Gavin was the eternal optimist in our family. He was always on the look-out for a silver lining - always willing to give the benefit of the doubt. He was our rock. He was our champion. We will keep fighting for Gavin and for every family faced with the pain of losing a loved one, followed by the devastating realization that the person who didn't have the decency to stop and help will be back living their life within months.

While we were not successful this time, we know there is hope here. We have seen it before and believe we can continue to convince legislators on both sides of the aisle that Gavin's Law is about people, not politics.

CHAPTER THIRTEEN
A FEW MORE LOVING MESSAGES

"The world has lost a great gift."
George – Student at Clovis West High School
Excerpt from He Loved Us

The first time Gary and I visited the crash site, besides picking up pieces of glass on the roadside, I found this beautiful note from Village members Wally, Urvi, and Zadien, tucked under a rock: Gavin, We love you so much. And will miss you every day until we meet again. We promise we will take care of Susan, Carter, and Isla. Keep an eye on us and know we will smile again... Love, W, U & Z

This Facebook post by a Bullard High School friend appeared the day after Gavin was killed, September 19, 2018: *Gavin Gladding, I sit here as tears fall from my eyes and questioning things...Words can't describe now how sad I feel for you and your family. The greatest man I've ever met and I'm glad I was friends with you for so long. I wish we could've spent more time together and for that I'm hurting so badly. Didn't know what to do so I went and put a cross of rocks for you. I'm struggling with this brother so please show me the path so I can better myself. When my time comes, we will meet again.*

That rock cross is still perfectly intact today as it was lovingly placed at the crash site in 2018.

A wooden, hand-hewn cross with his initials and the last words Gary said in his eulogy to Gavin "We'll go from here" also stands at the crash site. Another treasured gift made by our dear friend Ernie. I keep it surrounded all year round with colorful artificial flowers.

This email was sent to Darren's office on August 18, 2020: *I read with great disappointment that Gavin's Law failed to pass. My son was also killed by a hit-and-run driver 7 years ago, less than 2 weeks after his 22nd birthday. The driver was caught and sentenced to 5 years of probation. Please let me know what the next step is in keeping the case moving forward. And if I may assist in any way.*

Text message from our friend, Sandi, received Monday, September 7, 2020: *You honor your son every day, Rita. Gavin was highly regarded, esteemed by his peers and beloved by his family. Gone too soon but his memory lives in the hearts of those who knew him. All began with you and Gary, his mom and dad. We remember Gavin.*

The latest text message I received is from a friend of Gavin's elementary through high school years, that arrived February 27, 2022: "I know I speak for many that Gavin will be with us forever and continues to make us better."

On September 16, 2021, the third anniversary of the world's loss, Fort Washington Elementary school dedicated an area that looks out over the grounds behind the school. Named "The Gladding Gathering Place" benches were built to be used by all to just rest, and soak in one of Gavin's favorite vistas. With the entire school in attendance, a plaque was lovingly attached to the wall for all to see:

RITA GLADDING

The Gladding Gathering Area
in honor of
Mr. Gavin Gladding
Guidance Instructional Specialist
2016– 2018
"It's not where you go, it's who we meet along the way."
~The Wizard of Oz

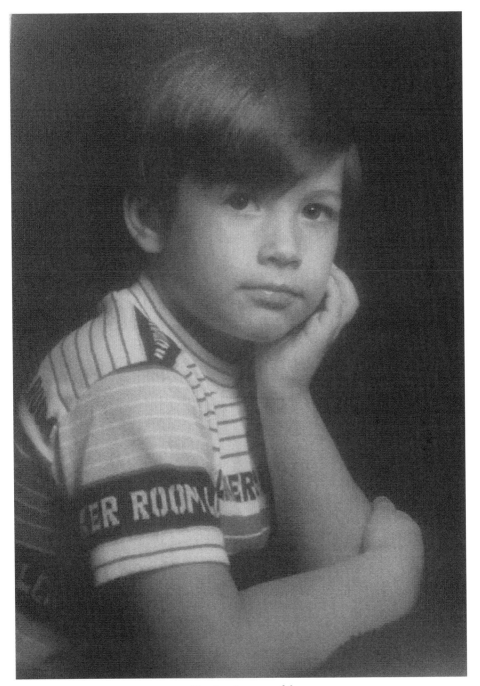

Gavin, 2 years old

Gavin during his years at University of Santa Barbara

Ft. Washington official 2018 photo taken two weeks before his death

AMBASSADORS

The writing of Gavin...Gone Turning Pain into Purpose to Create Legacy was simply an outpouring of love from my heart. It is Gavin's story simply put. I applaud each reader, especially my Ambassadors listed below, for creating the supportive environment that was essential for me to have the courage to deliver his story. For providing me this strength, I humbly thank each of the following Ambassadors.

My Family
Assemblyman Jim Patterson
Rhonda Parr Schafer
Samantha Pease Bauer
Annette Bozak
Darren Rose
Beverly McDonald
Armen Bacon
Joell Hallowell
Ralene Stevens
Flux Pilates & Wellness, Katie Anderson and Becky Gonzalez
Karen McCafferey
Paul and Kelly Lilles
Kim Negri
Paulin Sahakian
Mary Kay Buckley, LCSW

Catherine and Michael Jameson

Quigley Family

Melanie Warner

Todd and Kathy Spangler

Sutton Family

Corinne Peters

Bridgewealth Advisory Group, Joshua Carpenter, Partner

Jeff and Heidi Thomas

Danny Swaim

Joe and Kathy Talley

Mary Lynn Higginbotham

Keith and Susan Kraemer

Linda Glassman

Dean and Claudia Eller

Elizabeth and Blair Looney

Conner Houston

Polly Spangler-Bickell

Deanna and John Home

Leslie and Steve Botos

Dianna and Dick Kinsell

Maryann Ricchiuti

Linda Grossman

Suzy Ewell

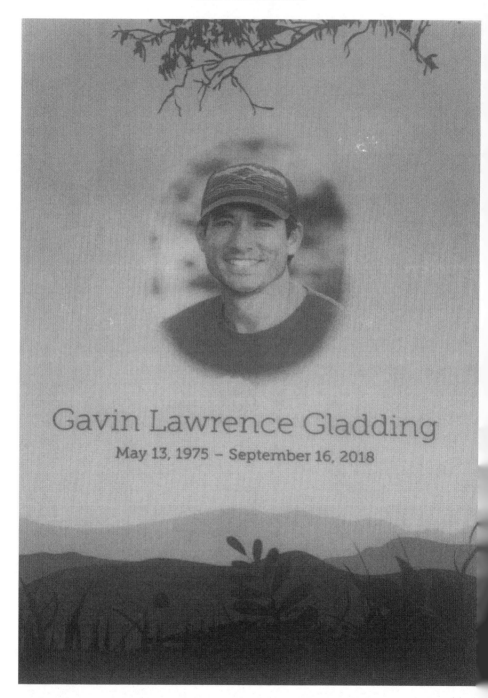

Gavin Lawrence Gladding

May 13, 1975 – September 16, 2018

About Defining Moments Press

Built for aspiring authors who are looking to share transformative ideas with others throughout the world, Defining Moments Press offers life coaches, healers, business professionals, and other non-fiction or self-help authors a comprehensive solution to getting their books published without breaking the bank or taking years.

Defining Moments Press prides itself on bringing readers and authors together to find tools and solutions.

As an alternative to self-publishing or signing with a major publishing house, we offer full profits to our authors, low-priced author copies, and simple contract terms.

Most authors get stuck trying to navigate the technical end of publishing. The comprehensive publishing services offered by Defining Moments Press mean that your book will be designed by an experienced graphic artist, available in printed, hard copy format, and coded for all eBook readers, including the Kindle, iPad, Nook, and more.

We handle all of the technical aspects of your book creation so you can spend more time focusing on your business that makes a difference for other people.

Defining Moments Press founder, publisher, and #1 bestselling author Melanie Warner has over 20 years of experience as a writer, publisher, master life coach, and accomplished entrepreneur.

You can learn more about Warner's innovative approach to self-publishing or take advantage of free trainings and education at: MyDefiningMoments.com.

Defining Moments Book Publishing

If you're like many authors, you have wanted to write a book for a long time, maybe you have even started a book...but somehow, as hard as you have tried to make your book a priority, other things keep getting in the way.

Some authors have fears about their ability to write or whether or not anyone will value what they write or buy their book. For others, the challenge is making the time to write their book or having accountability to finish it.

It's not just finding the time and confidence to write that is an obstacle. Most authors get overwhelmed with the logistics of finding an editor, finding a support team, hiring an experienced designer, and figuring out all the technicalities of writing, publishing, marketing, and launching a book. Others have actually written a book and might have even published it but did not find a way to make it profitable.

For more information on how to participate in our next Defining Moments Author Training program, visit: www.MyDefiningMoments.com. Or you can email melanie@MyDefiningMoments.com.

Other #1 Bestselling Books by Defining Moments Press

Defining Moments: Coping With the Loss of a Child - Melanie Warner

Defining Moments SOS: Stories of Survival - Melanie Warner and Amber Torres

Write your Bestselling Book in 8 Weeks or Less and Make a Profit - Even if No One Has Ever Heard of You - Melanie Warner

Become Brilliant: Roadmap From Fear to Courage – Shiran Cohen

Unspoken: Body Language and Human Behavior For Business - Shiran Cohen

Rise, Fight, Love, Repeat: Ignite Your Morning Fire - Jeff Wickersham

Life Mapping: Decoding the Blueprint of Your Soul - Karen Loenser

Ravens and Rainbows: A Mother-Daughter Story of Grit, Courage and Love After Death – L. Grey and Vanessa Lynn

Pivot You! 6 Powerful Steps to Thriving During Uncertain Times – Suzanne R. Sibilla

A Workforce Inspired: Tools to Manage Negativity and Support a Toxic-Free Workplace – Dolores Neira

Journey of 1000 Miles: A Musher and His Huskies' Journey on the Century-Old Klondike Trails - Hank DeBruin and Tanya McCready

7 Unstoppable Starting Powers: Powerful Strategies For Unparalled Results From Your First Year as a New Leader – Olusegun Eleboda

Bouncing Back From Divorce With Vitality & Purpose: A Strategy For Dads – Nigel J Smart, PHD

Focus on Jesus and Not the Storm: God's Non-negotiables to Christians in America - Keith Kelley

Stepping Out, Moving Forward: Songs and Devotions - Jacqueline O'Neil Kelley

Time Out For Time In: How Reconnecting With Yourself Can Help You Bond With Your Child in a Busy Word - Jerry Le

The Sacred Art of Off Mat Yoga: Whisper of Wisdom Forever – Shakti Barnhill

The Beauty of Change: The Fun Way For Women to Turn Pain Into Power & Purpose – Jean Amor Ramoran

From No Time to Free Time: 6 Steps to Work/Life Balance For Business Owners - Christoph Nauer

Self-Healing For Sexual Abuse Survivors: Tired of Just Surviving, Time to Thrive - Nickie V. Smith

Prepared Bible Study Lessons: Weekly Plans For Church Leaders - John W. Warner

Frog on a Lily Pad - Michael Lehre

How to Effectively Supercharge Your Career as a CEO - Giorgio Pasqualin

Rising From Unsustainable: Replacing Automobiles and Rockets - J.P. Sweeney

Food - Life's Gift for Healing: Simple, Delicious & Life Saving Whole Food Plant Based Solutions - Angel and Terry Grier

Harmonize All of You With All: The Leap Ahead in Self-Development - Artie Vipperla

Powerless to Powerful: How to Stop Living in Fear and Start Living Your Life - Kat Spencer

Living with Dirty Glasses: Heal with Empathy - Leah Montani

The Road Back to You: Finding Your Way After Losing a Child to Suicide - Trish Simonson

Made in the USA
Columbia, SC
03 July 2022

62637730R00093